# KITCHENER'S
# NEW ARMY

# KITCHENER'S NEW ARMY

## Your Country Needs You!

Edgar Wallace
edited by Campbell McCutcheon

AMBERLEY

First published 1915
This edition published 2015

Amberley Publishing
The Hill, Stroud
Gloucestershire, GL5 4EP

www.amberley-books.com

British Library Cataloguing in Publication Data.
A catalogue record for this book is available from the British Library.

ISBN 978 1 4456 2292 7 (print)
ISBN 978 1 4456 2306 1 (ebook)

Typeset in 10pt on 12pt Sabon.
Typesetting and Origination by Amberley Publishing.
Printed in the UK.

# Introduction

## PRELUDE TO WAR

The last two decades of the nineteenth century were ones of rampant expansion of Europe's superpowers. They saw the joining together of the various German states to become a unified Germany, as well as the rise in power of the British and the Austro-Hungarian empires. The industrialisation of Europe saw developments in weapons and in the ability to move people, and therefore troops, quickly as well as to provide the economic growth that helped fund the costs of each country's imperialist ambitions. The unification of Germany also saw a naval arms race like no other. From 1897 onwards, when Kaiser Wilhelm II saw the 168 vessels of the British fleet at the Diamond Jubilee Review at Spithead, both the German merchant and naval fleets saw a huge expansion. The UK was already the dominant sea power and did not want to see its position eroded. It was a case of keep up or lose command of the seas. In the age before aeroplanes, ships mattered.

The Kaiser had been furious that his paltry naval ships in attendance at Spithead were dwarfed by those not just of Britain, but of the USA and Russia too. He had witnessed from the deck of his royal yacht a British fleet that stretched 30 miles down the Solent. He had witnessed, too, the very first turbine steamer, a British invention, steam up and down at 30 knots past the fleet. It was all of this that made him decide Germany too would have such a navy, as powerful as the British, and that Germany too would be a major sea power as well as a major land power.

Within weeks of Spithead, Wilhelm II had promoted Admiral Alfred von Tirpitz to Secretary of State for the German Navy. Quickly, a plan was put together, now known as the Tirpitz Plan, to oversee a huge growth in the number and size of ships, and to create a navy so powerful that the Royal Navy would not want to fight it. After all, ships were hugely expensive and no one wanted to lose one.

Lord Kitchener, appointed minister of war on 5 August 1914, became the face of Britain's recruiting posters.

This was the first twentieth-century cold war, a period dedicated to war-mongering but without actually declaring hostilities. Britain's navy was spread throughout the world, defending British interests in Asia, Africa and the Americas, and Tirpitz surmised that the German navy need not be so big, just powerful enough to counter any British threats to it. His High Seas Fleet would be strong enough to simply prevent Britain's navy wanting to engage it. The first of many Acts passed through the German government in 1898, and soon the shipyards of Kiel, Bremerhaven, Stettin and Hamburg were busy with work, building not only battleships but also merchant ships. That period from 1900 onwards saw a series of German merchant vessels built that could compare with the best of Harland & Wolff or John Brown's and the fleets of Hamburg-Amerika and North German Lloyd dominated the Atlantic, winning the Blue Riband for Germany for the first time and with ships more opulent and luxurious than anything White Star or Cunard could offer.

With this huge German fleet under construction and all within hours of Britain's east coast, it was obvious Britain would have to compete. Admiral Jacky Fisher, the First Sea Lord, had decided Britain needed a fleet twice as large as Germany's within proximity to the North Sea. His forceful opinion that Britain needed a navy that was at least the size of the next two largest navies combined became accepted policy and Britain was soon building ships as fast as the shipyards could launch them.

At the same time, Germany's army was on a war footing too. That of Austro-Hungary was also being built up. Britain's army relied on highly trained and motivated regular soldiers, while the European armies relied on conscription, with many men having to do compulsory military service. One policy gave a motivated but small army which was well trained, while the alternative offered a vast group of men who had been trained militarily but were perhaps much less dedicated. With the expansion of their colonies, particularly in Africa, the European nations used their troops to protect their borders but also for this growth of their empires. Each imperialist expansion saw elements of gunboat diplomacy, with the British and French nearly clashing in Sudan in 1898, and, in 1911, the French and Germans almost coming to blows over parts of Morocco. With their territorial ambitions and a military build-up on the continent and in Britain, war was almost inevitable.

In 1906, Britain launched a new battleship, the *Dreadnought*. Massively heavily armed with ten 12-inch guns, armour plate and a top speed of 21.6 knots, she was more powerful than any ship afloat. The British turbine technology powered *Dreadnought* too. She was simply unbeatable. But Kaiser Wilhelm had decided that if Britain had *Dreadnought*, Germany would build similar, and so the arms race continued.

The father of *Dreadnought* was Admiral Jacky Fisher, who had asked soon after taking office for designs for a battleship with a top speed of 21 knots and armed mainly with 12-inch guns. At 18,120 tons, she was also among the largest naval ships afloat. With a length of 570 feet and a breadth of 82 feet 1 inch, and with five turrets of two 12-inch guns, she was simply revolutionary. Everything from her power plant to her armour was new. She was simply unbeatable. America was soon building Dreadnoughts, and Germany was too.

In 1905, *Dreadnought* had been laid down at Portsmouth and construction began. With three-bladed propellers and eighteen Babcock & Wilcox boilers powering her four turbines, she was faster than any battleship afloat, as well as better armoured and better gunned. With a range of some 6,620 miles she could travel the Atlantic and back without refuelling. She had electric range-finding equipment and was amazingly accurate for the time, with a range of over 13,000 yards. Her armour was German, however, mainly Krupp cemented armour.

With plans to have her built within a year, Fisher had stockpiled much of the steel required for her construction, as well as ordered boilers and engines. On 2 October 1905 she was laid down, and on 10 February 1906 she was launched by King Edward VII. It took four attempts to shatter the bottle of Australian wine used to name her. On 3 October 1906, she left on her sea trials and entered service on 11 December 1906, at a cost of £1,783,883. Her first voyage was to the Mediterranean and then she sailed for Trinidad in January 1907. Averaging 17 knots, she proved to be as good in real life as she was on paper. Returning to the UK, she became flagship for the Home Fleet and participated in the 1911 Coronation review.

As well as an expansion in new ships there was an expansion of naval bases too. For centuries the dominant threat to the UK had been from France and Spain. Now it was from Germany and the defences along the south coast were no longer as important. New naval bases, protecting the North Sea and the approaches to it from the Atlantic, were hastily built. Germany expanded its bases at Heligoland and at Kiel. The Kiel Canal had already given an easy access from the Baltic to the North Sea for the German fleet.

In 1908/09 German Dreadnought construction outpaced Britain's by seven to four. Britain's plans for just four Dreadnoughts in 1910–12 saw public outrage. Demonstrations saw the cry of 'we want eight and we won't wait' heard outside the Admiralty. The public got their way and eight were ordered. In 1911, five Dreadnoughts were being built. By 1913, as Britain was raising its number, German battleship construction was slowing down.

Both Britain and Germany were spending huge sums on their navies and it could not continue. The army had to be considered too; on land, things were changing also. Mechanisation, new weapons and new threats were all becoming rather important as the politics of Europe were taking a turn for the worse.

In 1914, Germany finally reached its two-thirds parity with Britain, having nineteen Dreadnoughts to Britain's twenty-nine.

In Britain, however, the desire to produce Dreadnoughts had caused a lack of investment in and new building of smaller naval vessels and many of the cruisers and destroyers were woefully inadequate for modern service. Germany had not ignored its smaller vessels and the German fleet was much more modern than Britain's, and, more importantly, the Germans had seen the advantage of submarines and had started construction of fleets of them too.

## POLITICAL ALLIANCES

Militarily, the major nations of Europe, Russia, France, Germany and Austria-Hungary, were preparing for war. The arms race could lead only one place, and with a militaristic regime in Germany, the other nations of Europe had to keep up. Along their borders, the peaceful Belgians built forts, as had the Germans and French. Politically, the countries allied themselves with neighbours and other nations. France was allied to Britain and Russia, Germany with the ethnically diverse Austro-Hungarian Empire and numerous smaller countries allied themselves with one or other of these factions. In the Balkans, both Russia and Austria-Hungary eyed the spoils of what was a splintering Turkish empire. Serbia would be the flashpoint of the war, although the events that started the chain reaction took place in Sarajevo, Bosnia, when Gavrilo Princip, a Bosnian Serb, assassinated Archduke Franz Ferdinand on 28 June 1914. Within the month, Austria-Hungary had made an ultimatum to the Serbs. Ten demands were made and Serbia agreed to nine, while mobilizing her armed forces at the same time. Austria-Hungary refused this compromise and declared war on Serbia on 28 July. Russia came down on the side of the Serbs, while Germany supported the Austro-Hungarians. Britain mobilized and ordered its naval vessels to their war bases. On 29 July, the first shots were fired by the Austro-Hungarian navy against Belgrade. The war had begun and it was expected to be a short one.

## THE WAR BEGINS

With the assassination of Archduke Franz Ferdinand in Sarajevo, the fate of Europe was decided. In a series of political machinations, country after country declared war against each other. At the end of July, the German fleet was recalled from its Norwegian exercises and on 1 August, the British battle fleets were ordered to war stations. On 4 August 1914, war was declared between Britain and Germany. Admiral Sir John Jellicoe was made commander of the Grand

Fleet. A blockade was made of German shipping, from the Dover Patrol in the Channel to the Grand Fleet in the North Sea. Ships were stopped, prizes taken and contraband in neutral ships confiscated. German merchant ships at sea were quickly converted into armed merchant cruisers or made mercy dashes for neutral and home ports. Even the *Mauretania*, the world's fastest ship, made for Halifax, Nova Scotia, before a high-speed dash across the Atlantic to Liverpool. Germany's *Kronprinzessin Cecile* was interred at Bar Harbor in Maine, and the port of Falmouth soon filled with prizes of war.

Germany declared war on neutral Belgium on 4 August. The coalfields of Belgium would be an excellent addition to German resources, but, more importantly, the German army needed to cross Belgium to take northern France and open the route to Paris. The Schlieffen Plan, as it was known, would see the Germans attack on a front that extended from Belgium to Luxembourg. The plan would be to knock France out before it mobilized, while turning on Russia after the French had capitulated.

On the first day of war, the German battleship *Goeben* and the cruiser *Breslau* were detected by HMS *Gloucester*, using radio transmissions to find them. The ships ran for Constantinople, shelling Bone and Philippeville on the way. France was at war but Britain wasn't yet, so when the ships were spotted by *Indomitable* and *Indefatigable* they let them pass. Soon the two German ships had slipped into the Dardanelles and headed for Constantinople. The two German ships were quickly 'sold' to the Turks. No one was fooled by the German crew in Turkish uniforms, but as Turkey was neutral nothing could be done.

The first British shots of the war were fired on the 5th by the destroyer *Lance*, which sank the German minelayer *Konigen Luise* in the Thames estuary. The next day saw the first British casualty when the cruiser *Amphion* was sunk by one of *Konigen Luise*'s mines. Her captain ordered 'Abandon Ship' but she hit another mine before finally sinking, taking nineteen German survivors of the *Konigen Luise* to the bottom.

A day later, but a world away in the West Indies, the cruiser *Suffolk* came upon the cruiser *Karlsruhe* and the liner *Kronprinz Wilhelm* transferring guns and supplies. The *Kronprinz Wilhelm* had been built to be converted into an armed merchant cruiser and the guns were destined for her. *Suffolk* quickly began the chase of *Karlsruhe* but lost the faster German vessel. 100 miles north of the Orkneys, on the 9th, the light cruiser *Birmingham* sank the first U-boat of the war, the *U-15*. On the 26th, after a short chase, the armed merchant cruiser *Kaiser Wilhelm der Grosse*, once Germany's fastest merchant vessel and the first of the fifteen four-funnelled liners built, was cornered by HMS *Highflyer* off the west coast of Africa. The German ship was attacked and within an hour was on her side and sinking. Ninety of her crew reached shore before she went to the bottom. She was the first armed merchant cruiser of the war to be lost to enemy action.

## KITCHENER'S CALL TO ARMS

On land, war continued apace. British troops were mobilized for the defence of Belgium, while Serbia declared war on Germany on 6 August. On the 8th, Lord Kitchener called for 100,000 volunteers to take up arms against Germany, which had violated Belgian neutrality. By 10 August, Liege's first forts had fallen to the Germans and on 12 August, Britain declared war on Austria-Hungary. On 14 August, H. G. Wells called the conflict 'the war to end all wars'. Between 14–22 August the French, as expected by the Germans, attacked Alsace-Lorraine, which they had lost in the Franco-Prussian War. On 16 August, Liege surrendered. The next day, the Russians invaded East Prussia. In a fast-moving conflict on the 18th, the Belgian army retreated to Antwerp and, on the 19th, the German army shot 150 civilians at Aerschot. Brussels was occupied on the 20th while fighting continued in East Prussia, the Cameroons were invaded by the British, with some 400 troops and the German high command authorized the use of Zeppelins against London and other British targets.

In the Ardennes, a French army was almost wiped out in fierce fighting with the Germans and the French fell back to a defensive line along the rivers Meuse and Marne. On 23 August, the Japanese declared war against Germany and Austria-Hungary. Their targets were clearly the German treaty ports in China, including Tsingtao. The Battle of Mons took place too, with the small, but well-trained and equipped British Expeditionary Force taking part for the first time. Despite their accurate fire, the British had to withdraw, making an orderly retreat. Some 300,000 French casualties had been killed or wounded in the first clashes of the war. The Austro-Hungarians attacked Russian-controlled Poland on 23 August, creating a diversion for the Germans fighting in East Prussia. In the Battle of Tannenberg, the Germans captured almost 100,000 Russians. In Togoland, on 26 August, the British and French captured the colony from the Germans.

On 28 August, the British battlecruisers *Invincible*, *Lion*, *New Zealand*, *Princess Royal* and *Queen Mary*, under Admiral David Beatty attacked a German fleet in what was to become the Battle of the Heligoland Bight. A light cruiser force had left Harwich to force the Germans into action. The plan worked and the German force was ambushed with the loss of three cruisers, the *Ariadne*, *Köln* and *Mainz*, and a destroyer. With just thirty-five casualties, the British fleet took 1,000 prisoners.

On 30 August, Paris was bombed from the air, making it the first capital city to be attacked this way. A German Taube fighter dropped four small bombs as well as propaganda leaflets.

Disaster befell the Austro-Hungarian forces in Galicia and it was obvious they could not fight a modern war without German help. In September came the first loss to a U-boat of the war when HMS *Pathfinder* was sunk by *U-21* off the Isle of May on the 5th. Eight days later, Lt Cmdr Max Horton in *E9* sank the German cruiser *Hela* off Heligoland. Horton would go onto great success as a submarine captain. Also on the 5th, the British and French counter-attacked along the Marne. The first battle here was known as the Battle of the Ourcq and it caused a gap to open between Kluck's First Army and von Bülow's Second Army, which the British exploited. On the 9th, the Germans began to withdraw after suffering heavy casualties. It was this defeat that ultimately led to the failure of the Schlieffen Plan. The failure to capture Paris and knock out the French would have disastrous consequences for tens of millions of men, women and children in Europe. With this defeat came the prospect of the Germans fighting on two fronts. With Antwerp under attack, King Albert of the Belgians counterattacked, causing the Germans to bring more soldiers and artillery to the city. British naval forces also took part in the defence of Antwerp. A German army, after soundly defeating the Russians, was rushed to Silesia to help the Austro-Hungarians on 17 September.

On 19 September, the German cruiser *Königsberg*, which had been hiding in the Rufiji delta, decided to attack. Her port of call was Zanzibar, where she sank HMS *Pegasus*. The 22nd saw the SMS *Emden* begin her war career proper in the Indian Ocean, when she bombarded the oil refinery at Madras. She was to sink many vessels before being caught by HMS *Sydney*. Britain's major defeat of the early war was to come on the 22nd, when the *Aboukir*, *Hogue* and *Cressy*, three rather old and outdated cruisers, were to be sunk by the *U-9*. The neglect of the smaller cruisers and the emphasis on Dreadnoughts was to cost dear: 1,459 sailors died that day. *Aboukir* was hit first and the two other ships torpedoed while attempting to rescue survivors.

October saw the Royal Naval Division take part in the final defence of Antwerp and the Royal Naval Air Service attack the Zeppelin hangers at Dusseldorf on the 8th. Seven days later, HMS *Hawke* was sunk by *U-9*. The first Canadian troops arrived in Plymouth on 13 October while on the 17th, the light cruiser *Undaunted* and four destroyers sank four German destroyers off Texel. New Zealand troops left Wellington for Britain on 16 October. This influx of troops from the Empire continued through 1915 too and was an early sign of the need for many thousands of new troops. Conscription saw the potential of the small British army to be overwhelmed by the standing armies of Germany, Austria-Hungary and their allies. The next day, some 20,000 Australian troops left for the UK too. Parts of low-lying Belgium were flooded to prevent the Germans advancing. War in the Middle East began with the invasion of Mesopotamia by British Indian troops on 23 October. The Turks were finally forced out of Basra on 23 November.

The heavily gunned but lightly built monitors *Humber*, *Severn* and *Mersey* were used to bombard the Belgian coast on the 18th; the next day saw the *E9* lost to a U-boat and on the 20th the first British merchant ship of the war lost to a submarine was the *Glitra*, sunk by *U-17*. Mined on the next day was the virtually brand-new Dreadnought HMS *Audacious*. She was mortally wounded and, despite efforts to tow her to safety, blew up and sank at 11.00 p.m. that night. The Admiralty tried to pretend she had not been sunk but many Americans had been aboard the White Star liner *Olympic*, which had spent much of the early evening rescuing her crew. The end of October saw the discovery of the *Königsberg* in the Rufuji delta and attempts were made to flush her out.

Between 29 October and 24 November, heavy fighting around Ypres ended in stalemate and the troops began to dig in for a long war, with trenches ultimately being constructed between the North Sea and the Swiss border. Any hope of a quick end to the war was pretty much over and troops would be needed in their hundreds of thousands.

November saw the search for the East Asiatic Squadron of Admiral von Spee. The light cruiser HMS *Glasgow* and two rather old cruisers, the *Monmouth* and *Good Hope*, along with the Orient Line's *Otranto*, converted to a lightly defended armed merchant cruiser, began the search. They were soon joined by the pre-Dreadnought HMS *Canopus*, which was slow and had never fired a gun in anger. On the first, the two fleets met at Coronel, Chile. Within the hour the two older cruisers were gone, lost with all hands, and with no damage to the German fleet at all. Britain had suffered its first naval defeat in a century and with the loss of two entire crews too.

Russia declared war on Turkey on 2 November and invaded Turkish-held Armenia. The Turks repulsed the attack on 11 November. On the 3rd, in East Africa, the British failed to capture German-held Tanga. In Britain, the Norfolk and Suffolk coast was bombarded by the Germans on 3 November while on the 7th, von Spee's base at Tsingtao was captured. That same day, Turkey declared war on little Belgium. Two days later, there was more good news for the Allies when the *Emden* was sunk by HMS *Sydney*. She had been cornered while attempting to shell the wireless station on the Cocos Islands. *Emden* had been responsible for the loss of almost thirty merchant ships, as well as several battleships of the French and Russian navies. The next day, plans were set in motion to sink the *Königsberg*. A collier, the *Newbridge*, was sunk across the Rufiji estuary and the *Königsberg* was trapped. It was only a matter of time before larger British ships could come and bombard the German ship and sink her. 746 members of the crew of HMS *Bulwark* died when she exploded at Sheerness while taking on ammunition on the 26th.

December saw *Invincible* and *Inflexible* arrive at Port Stanley on the 7th and engage von Spee's battle fleet the next day. It was a resounding victory for the British navy. *Scharnhorst*, *Gneisenau*, *Nürnberg* and *Leipzig* were all sunk and only the *Dresden* evaded the British fleet. The Balkans campaign saw some

170,000 Serbian casualties, out of an army of 400,000. The Battle of Kolubra saw the Austro-Hungarian army thrown out of Serbia. The Austro-Hungarians suffered over 50 per cent casualties, with some 230,000 dead or injured.

Admiral Hipper brought a large force of ships out on the 15th and proceeded to bombard England's east coast. From Hartlepool to Whitby and Scarborough, a huge amount of damage was caused, and it was feared that German waiters in the seaside resorts had given the German navy clues as to what to bombard. Even Whitby Abbey was hit by shells and many homes and businesses were destroyed in the Yorkshire towns. Some 120 people were killed during and after the shelling. The shellings were a great propaganda coup for the British army, which used it to encourage more men to join for the duration of the war. On Christmas Day, Cuxhaven was bombed by the RNAS and the German fleet was forced to disperse along the banks of the Kiel Canal. It was the last major event of the naval war of 1914.

Despite fighting in the Champagne region, the armies had dug in for a long war, and all was quiet on the Western Front. The casualty figures had a great deal to do with it and all sides needed to regroup and rearm. In less than six months, over 1 million Britons, French and Belgians had become casualties. The German losses on the Western Front were some 675,000 with another 275,000 dead or wounded on the Eastern Front. 1 million Austro-Hungarians and 1.8 million Russians were also dead or wounded. 25 December, Christmas Day, saw an uneasy truce in parts of the Western Front, with German and British soldiers playing football in no man's land. They would go back to their trenches, realizing the enemy was just like them, and dig in for the duration. The rest of the war would be a long, hard slog, in mud and difficult conditions, but for one day, the soldiers had some respite from the horrors of war. And so ended the first year of a war that everyone thought would be over for Christmas.

## WHO WAS KITCHENER?

Field Marshall Horatio Herbert Kitchener, 1st Earl Kitchener, had foreseen the length of the war and before it was over a month, he was already requesting that more men join up. But who was Kitchener?

Born on 24 June 1850, in Ballylongford, County Kerry, Kitchener was educated in Montreaux and then at the Royal Military College. He joined the French army during the Franco-Prussian War in a field ambulance unit but returned to the UK after catching pneumonia after watching the French Army of the Loire from a balloon. Reprimanded upon his return, for breaking neutrality, he served in Palestine, Egypt and Cyprus as a surveyor. By this time he was an officer in the Royal Engineers. By 1879, after a time in Cyprus, he was vice-consul in

Anatolia. He moved from there to Egypt in 1883 and was promoted to captain. By 1888, he had become brevet colonel and major in 1889. He led the Egyptian cavalry at the Battle of Toski in that year and became adjutant-general of the Egyptian army in December 1890. He then became Sirdar of the Egyptian army in 1892, effectively being the commander-in-chief. He became a major-general after the Battle of Hafir, also becoming a household name in Britain at the same time. He was victorious in the Battle of Omdurman in 1898, too. He became Baron of Khartoum in October 1898, the month after he became governor-general of Sudan. During the Boer War, Kitchener arrived in South Africa on the RMS *Dunottar Castle*, one of the first troopships carrying reinforcements, in December 1899 as chief of staff, effectively second in command. He was at the Relief of Kimberley and led the unsuccessful British forces at the Battle of Paardeberg in February 1900. He tried to calm some of the excesses demanded by the British leaders after victory over the Boers, having managed to create peace in the Sudan with similar techniques. After his successes in South Africa, Kitchener was promoted to commander-in-chief of the army in India and quickly set about reorganizing the Indian troops. Britain, with its small standing army, was reliant on its overseas Dominions to provide troops when necessary, and Kitchener was preparing for war, by reducing the size of fixed garrisons, and reorganizing it into two more mobile armies.

In 1909, Kitchener was made field marshal and went on a tour of New Zealand and Australia. In 1911, he returned again to Egypt after turning down the post of C-in-C in the Mediterranean and being turned down for the job of Viceroy of India. At the start of the First World War, Kitchener was recalled to London by Prime Minister Asquith and became secretary of state for war. Cabinet opinion was that the war would be a short one, but Kitchener estimated it would last a minimum of three years. Huge new armies would be required and Kitchener expected casualties to be massive. He made the call soon after becoming secretary of state, with the *London Opinion*'s artist, Alfred Leete, making a special cover for the newspaper showing Kitchener pointing at the reader, with the words 'Britons [Kitchener] wants YOU, Join your Country's Army!' underneath. This image has become one of the most recognizable of any war.

The 'New Armies' created would come into action in 1916, after months of training. Cabinet Secretary Maurice Hankey, impressed with Kitchener's skills, said this of him:

> The great outstanding fact is that within eighteen months of the outbreak of the war, when he had found a people reliant on sea-power, and essentially non-military in their outlook, he had conceived and brought into being, completely equipped in every way, a national army capable of holding its own against the armies of the greatest military Power the world had ever seen.

Kitchener began the war with a tiny but well-trained British army. His plan was that the British should not be brought into action until the intentions of the Germans had been worked out. He foresaw an attack at Amiens, with the British not going into Belgium at all, as the Belgian army would soon be overrun and the British would lose their equipment in any rout. Kitchener wanted Britain to preserve her men and materiel as the war would be a long one. As such, he only sent four divisions to France, keeping two in reserve. It was a sensible precaution. The British Expeditionary Force was made up of only 100,000 men, half of them regular troops, the other half reservists. This was Britain's army at the time, all of it, and Kitchener did not want to lose it unnecessarily. Facing them were hundreds of thousands of Germans and it was the sad realization that Britain was woefully lacking in trained soldiers, having spent much of its money pre-war building up the navy to the detriment of the army, that saw Kitchener begin the recruiting process that would see a ten-fold increase in the army and over 1 million men in uniform by 1916.

Many of the British Army's leaders wanted the New Army battalions to be integrated into the army divisions, but Kitchener wanted them to stand alone as divisions in their own rights. These battalions were formed by locality or trade, the idea being that men would join up from peer pressure, remaining with their friends throughout the war, creating an instant camaraderie that would bind each battalion together. In reality it created groups of neighbours who, when they entered the conflict, would be mown down on the fields of France, with streets and neighbourhoods bearing the brunt of casualties when each battalion entered the fray. If these men had been sent into existing divisions, and spread around, they would still have suffered the same casualties but they would not be so pronounced, as happened at the Battle of the Somme in 1916.

Kitchener had realized that the Western Front trenches were effectively a siege line and that the war would be fought over a small strip of land in France and Belgium. He wanted to create a second front that would distract the Germans and their allies. He wanted to attack the Turks at Alexandrette, the centre of the Ottoman railway network, but was drawn into the disastrous Gallipoli campaign instead. Kitchener was involved in the shell crisis of 1915 and he slowly began to see his power and influence reduced. Kitchener attempted to preserve his New Army until 1916, when he foresaw a triumphant victory over the Germans, and tried to prevent their use in France in 1915. By August 1915, some battalions were moved to France and took part in the Battle of Loos in September. The French were worried the Russians would sue for peace and the battle was seen as a way of removing pressure from the Eastern Front. By late 1915, Kitchener was being blamed for not introducing conscription and his power was firmly on the wane. Volunteering was failing to provide the numbers for a seventy-division British army. In early 1916 Kitchener lost much of his power, and he was considered tired and that his mind was losing comprehension. Much effort was being taken up by the planning for the Battle of the Somme, but Kitchener was also being called to account for the lack of supplies coming from the USA. Some 2 million rifles had been ordered but, by June 1916, fewer than 500 had been delivered.

Kitchener had planned to sail to Russia on a diplomatic mission in June 1916. He would sail from Scapa Flow on HMS *Hampshire*. Built at Elswick on the Tyne by Armstrong Whitworth, and launched on 24 September 1903, HMS *Hampshire* was a Devonshire class armoured cruiser. She spent her early career from 1905 with the Channel Fleet, before heading for the Mediterranean in 1911 and then onto the China Station. At the start of the war, she was sent back to Britain and joined the Grand Fleet at Scapa in 1915. On 31 May 1916, she took part in the Battle of Jutland and returned to Scapa afterwards. She was soon ordered to head for Archangel in Russia, with Lord Kitchener aboard. Escorted by the destroyers *Unity* and *Victor*, she set sail at 4.45 p.m. on the afternoon of 5 June 1916 into a heavy gale, which soon strengthened. Assuming no submarines would be operating, HMS *Hampshire*'s commanding officer, Captain Savill, ordered the destroyers to return to Scapa.

Riding heavy seas, *Hampshire* continued alone on her secret mission to Russia and was soon passing Marwick Head. At 7.40 p.m., an explosion caused her to heel to starboard. Within fifteen minutes, with her lifeboats on the starboard side damaged by the weather and the explosion and those on port side unable to be launched, she sank by the bow and was lost with all but twelve of her crew of over 600. It is thought that *Hampshire* had been sunk by mines laid immediately prior to Jutland by the submarine mine-layer *U-75*. Claims were made by a German spy that he had sabotaged the *Hampshire* and that he had escaped from the ship immediately prior to her sinking. *Hampshire* and her crew, as well as Kitchener and his staff, were lost and the wreck lies in 65 metres of water. Despite it being illegal to dive on her, a propeller and shaft were removed. They now reside at Lyness as a monument to the men who lost their lives.

Kitchener died at sea as his beloved New Army was committed at the Battle of the Somme. He would die before he saw the tragic waste of the hundreds of thousands of men who had answered his call to arms in August 1914.

These men had spent much of 1914 and 1915 training for their entry into the war. Kitchener's Army would make a huge effect on the conflict and many tens of thousands would pay with their lives. The forthcoming pages, written by the co-author of the screenplay of *King Kong*, tell the story of Kitchener's Army, written at a time when they had yet to enter the conflict, showing the men as they went from raw recruits to finished soldiers. The bonhomie is evident, as is the jovial nature of the training. It would hardly have prepared them for the battle they would face in the mud of Flanders and in the heat of the Dardanelles.

The forthcoming pages do give a realistic idea of how our grandfathers, great-grandfathers and great-great-grandfathers were trained. It unfortunately does not tell us how they died. Many of the men shown in the following pages did not survive the war, but this is a fitting tribute to the Pal's Battalions and the hundreds of thousands of them who perished and for whom a foreign field is their resting place.

## RECRUITING

At the outbreak of the First World War, Britain's confidence in its naval superiority and the protection offered by its waters had left the nation unprepared for a drawn-out land war. The army consisted of around 710,000 men including reserves, of which only 80,000 were regular troops, trained and ready to fight. This was far less than either the German or French armies. The British Army was made up of six divisions and one cavalry division within the UK, and a further four divisions overseas. There were also fourteen Territorial Force divisions, plus 300,000 men in the Reserves. The secretary of state for war, Lord Kitchener, feared that the untrained Territorials would be ineffectual and despite the popular feeling that it would be 'all over by Christmas', he anticipated a far longer and drawn-out war. More men and, as the posters would later state, yet more men were needed. However the British did not use conscription for overseas conflicts, and at first all of the extra men were volunteers, encouraged to enlist through the persuasive propaganda of the time and, in no small measure, by the countless recruiting posters that beckoned and pointed on every street, as well as peer pressure from friends, colleagues and family.

In an age long before television, the posters were the most immediate means of mass communication available, especially with their target audience, the mostly illiterate or semi-literate men of the working classes who did more than their share to feed the machinery of war. Advertising posters were well established throughout the towns and cities, and while the British style of posters might have lacked the artistic qualities of their French counterparts, or the graphic boldness of the German posters, their slogans and simple imagery were easily and instantly understood by the general public. For the initial period they were fairly innocuous appeals or calls to action, inviting the men to enlist to 'answer the call'. It was all about duty and pride as the flow of civilians seamlessly became ranks of khaki-clad soldiers. Smiling faces abounded beneath slogans such as, 'Come along boys!' Another featured a smiling Tommy and the wording, 'He's happy and satisfied – are you?'

An initial wave of enthusiasm saw 750,000 men enlist by the end of September 1914, rising to a million by the end of the year. Their reasons for joining up were many and varied and while no doubt some were prompted by unemployment and poverty at home, the recruiting boom did not subside in the wake of the British retreat following the Battle of Mons. Voluntary enlistment continued until the introduction of compulsory conscription in January 1916.

### A WASTE OF GOOD MATERIAL.

BRITANNIA (to LORD KITCHENER). "WELCOME BACK! I WISH A BETTER POST COULD HAVE BEEN FOUND FOR YOU—BUT OUR POLITICIANS ARE A LITTLE AFRAID OF STRONG MEN."

[Lord Kitchener's new post is the Mediterranean military command. Its last occupant resigned on the ground that it didn't give him enough employment.]

### REINFORCED CONCRETE.

JOHN BULL. "IF YOU NEED ASSURANCE, SIR, YOU MAY LIKE TO KNOW THAT YOU HAVE THE LOYAL SUPPORT OF ALL DECENT PEOPLE IN THIS COUNTRY."

Two cartoons, from 1910 and 1914, featuring the rise of Lord Kitchener.

Lord Kitchener addresses an enthusiastic crowd at a recruiting rally.

Lord Kitchener, the poster boy of the First World War, although in recent years there has been some dispute concerning whether Alfred Leete's design for *London Opinion* actually appeared as a recruiting poster.

## DERBY'S DAY.

### WITH MR. PUNCH'S COMPLIMENTS TO THE DIRECTOR OF RECRUITING.

The Derby scheme, named after Lord Derby, encouraged men to 'attest' their intention to enlist. Under the 'group scheme', it encouraged groups of men from a particular area to enlist and fight together in the so-called Pals' Battalions.

In White City Central Depot a group of 'Derby men' hand in their armlets in exchange for a full uniform.

Playing the game

At the start of the war there had been a push by the professional football clubs to carry on playing in order to keep people's spirits up. However, this backfired when public opinion openly turned against the football clubs. In 1914 Arthur Conan Doyle, the creator of Sherlock Holmes, made a direct appeal to footballers to volunteer for military service. 'If a footballer has strength of limb, let them serve and march in the field of battle.' Many footballers, and other sportsmen, heeded the call and a special Football Battalion was formed as a Pals Battalion within the Middlesex Regiment. During the war the regiment lost more than a thousand men.

*Above and below:* Recruiting poster aimed at Rugby Union players, and a cartoon from *Punch*: 'Mr Punch (to Professional Association Player). No doubt you can make money in this field, my friend, but there's only one field where you can get honour.'

'Play the Greater Game and Join the Football Battalion'. Recruiting poster depicting a very basic form of trench warfare.

'The fortunes of war.' The London offices of the Hamburg-Amerika Line transformed into a British recruiting office in 1914.

Crowds of young men gather outside a recruiting office, eager to do their bit for king and country.

What appears to be a familiar scene outside a recruiting office, but it actually features members of the Royal Highlanders in Canada. Thousands of Brits living overseas, as well as members of the Empire nations, were called to bear arms, and they came in their thousands.

This watch factory in Prescot was turned into the barracks for the local Pals battalion.

Lord Roberts is cheered by new recruits of Kitchener's Second Army in Temple Gardens, London. A national hero, Lord Roberts had won the VC in 1858 during the Indian Mutiny. Roberts himself died in November 1914.

Soon, soldiers were being trained in hastily created camps all over the country. Buildings were taken over for barracks, such as the watch factory in Prescot, Lancashire, but most training initially took place in basic camps, with tents for accommodation.

Honourable Artillery Company recruits at Aldershot – note the rag-tag uniforms and footwear. It would take time for the army to manage to provide uniforms for all new recruits and huge effort was required on the Home Front to manufacture enough khaki cloth for uniforms. These men would be looking after the horses and the guns of the HAC.

Honourable Artillery Company recruits are given instruction on their weapon of choice, the QF 15-pounder gun. Purchased from Germany in 1900, these guns were a stopgap to replace the obsolete British weapons that had been shown to be inadequate against more modern guns supplied by France and Germany to the Boers. B-Battery of the HAC used these weapons in anger in Aden in 1915.

Hastily dug trenches were built all over the UK so soldiers could be given a flavour of life on the Western Front. Of course, unlike in France, the soldiers could go back to a nice warm barracks after a day of mock fighting.

Bread ovens – the army marches on its stomach.

King George V inspecting troops. The king would make numerous visits to the Front during the course of the war.

A "SAMPLE" OF NEW ARM[Y]

MAKING SOLDIERS OF 3,000,000 MEN IN 12 MONTHS

*Above and below:* In a year of hard training some three million men had been put into uniform, trained and were now ready to fight. Some were sent to far-flung parts of the Empire so that the regular troops could be released for active service. Little did some of these men know that they would be slaughtered in the trenches within months of finishing their training. The first battalions were ready to enter service in summer 1915 and the next wave were ready in time for the Battle of the Somme, in 1916, which would see tens of thousands of men killed each day in a futile attempt to break through the German lines.

Oakley, Photo, Copyright,    Troops at Sonthampton.    Netley, Southampton

Soldiers aboard a troopship. Britain had the world's largest merchant navy and could call up many vessels to use when her troops needed to be mobilised. This view, taken at Southampton, shows troops probably on their way to France.

## MARINES LANDING IN FRANCE.

Marines landing in France, August 1914. The Royal Naval Division was rushed to Belgium to try and prevent the fall of Liège and Antwerp. Britain's Royal Naval Division eventually became a major component of the British Army, fighting on all fronts from the Dardanelles to the Western Front.

Men of the Royal Naval Division in training at the Crystal Palace, Sydenham, south London. The Royal Naval Division became a major component of the British Army.

This clever ruse was used to make men join the Royal Naval Division. The display had a mirror in which the raw recruit could see the kind of man the Navy wanted. Of course, it was his own reflection in the mirror.

# ROYAL NAVAL DIVISION

## HANDYMEN TO FIGHT ON LAND & SEA

### 1ST BRIGADE

BATTALIONS:

"BENBOW"
"COLLINGWOOD"
"HAWKE"
"DRAKE"

## RECRUITS WANTED

### 2ND BRIGADE

BATTALIONS:

"HOWE"
"HOOD"
"ANSON"
"NELSON"

## RECRUITS WANTED

VACANCIES FOR RECRUITS BETWEEN THE AGES OF 18 AND 38
CHEST MEASUREMENT, 34 in.    HEIGHT, 5 ft. 3½ in.
PAYMENT FROM 1/3 PER DAY.  FAMILY ALLOWANCES.

Besides serving in the above Battalions and for the Transport
and Engineer Sections attached,

# MEN WANTED

who are suitable for training as Wireless Operators,
Signalmen, and other Service with the Fleet.
Apply to the Recruiting Office, 112, STRAND, LONDON, W.C.

The poster seen in the image opposite was this one. It worked a treat as many thousands joined the RND as a direct result of the recruiting campaigns in 1914. Soon, the RND was greatly expanded to include numerous battalions named after famous admirals such as Drake, Hawke, Howe and Nelson.

'Off to the Front.' During the war the women did far more than just pack their men off to fight. However, this is a recurring theme of the pre-enlistment recruiting posters at the beginning of the war.

It wasn't just the wives and girlfriends who did their duty. Mothers were also urged to send off their sons, as depicted in this poster.

'Take Up the Sword of Justice' became the slogan following the sinking of the *Lusitania*. The stricken ship and many of its unfortunate passengers are depicted in the background on this poster.

*Above and right:* The sinking of the *Lusitania* coloured public opinion on both sides of the Atlantic and the incident became a rallying point for the recruiting campaign.

*Above:* A recruiting sergeant in Bermondsey refers to a poster featuring the ocean liner.

*Right:* Under a banner headline, 'Remember the *Lusitania*', this poster remonstrates against 'this devil's work'.

# REMEMBER THE
# LUSITANIA

THE JURY'S VERDICT SAYS:
"We find that the said deceased died from their prolonged immersion and exhaustion in the sea eight miles south south-west of the Old Head of Kinsale on Friday, May 7th, 1915, owing to the sinking of the R.M.S. Lusitania by a torpedo fired without warning from a German submarine."

"That this appalling crime was contrary to international law and the conventions of all civilized nations, and we therefore charge the officers of the said submarine, the Emperor and Government of Germany, under whose orders they acted, with the crime of wilful and wholesale murder before the tribunal of the civilized world."

*IT IS YOUR DUTY TO TAKE UP THE SWORD OF JUSTICE TO AVENGE THIS DEVIL'S WORK.*

# ENLIST TO-DAY

THE SOLDIER AND THE MUNITION-WORKER.
"WE'RE BOTH NEEDED TO SERVE THE GUNS!"
[*With acknowledgments to a popular poster.*]

*Above and left:* 'We're both needed to serve the guns,' states the poster, top. It provided the inspiration for this *Punch* cartoon (left) published in June 1915, with the design adapted to reflect the nation's gratitude to the munitions minister, Lloyd George, following the debacle of the Shell Scandal.

THE
# SPORTSMAN BATTALION'S
# RECRUIT
## WHO WRECKED THE ZEPPELIN
### and won the V.C.

By permission of F. M. Birkett and The "Daily Sketch."

# FOLLOW HIS LEAD
## AND JOIN THE
# SPORTSMAN'S BATTALION

Apply E. CUNLIFFE-OWEN, Hotel Cecil, Strand, London,

W. STRAKER, Ltd., Printers, 13, Coventry Street, Piccadilly, W.

In January 1915 the Kaiser had reluctantly given permission for raids on England, but stipulated that they were to be against military targets and that London was to be excluded. Following the raids on the Norfolk coast in January, when two airships targeting the Humber were blown off course, the bombing of London's docks was authorised in the following month. On 31 May 1915, the LZ 38 made the first raid on London, dropping 120 bombs on the capital. What the British needed was a victory against the raiders.

This came on 15 June 1915, when Reginald Warneford of the Royal Naval Air Service, shown above, flying in a Morane-Saulnier monoplane, brought down the LZ 37 near Ghent. Warneford was awarded the VC for his actions, but they were eclipsed in September 1916 when Captain William Leefe Robinson downed the Shutte-Lanz airship SL 11 over Cuffley in Hertfordshire. Poster depicting Warneford, although he is not mentioned by name.

Kitchener inspecting troops at the Guildhall in London, 1915.

*Above and below:* Kitchener addresses an enthusiastic crowd outside London's Guildhall after a recruiting speech calling for 'yet more men'. Many of these came from the dominions and, below, the High Commissioner for Australia is seen inspecting a contingent of his countrymen.

The British launched a limted offensive at Neuve-Chapelle in Artois, north-eastern France, on 10 March 1915. British and Indian forces made good progress until German counterattacks halted their advance. They dug in but under heavy bombardment suffered more than 11,500 casualties. They learned the hard way that in future, artillery fire was the only way to break through the trenches. This famous poster is by the celebrated Welsh artist Frank Brangwyn.

## OUR FRIEND THE ENEMY.

John Bull (*very calmly*). "AH, HERE HE COMES AGAIN—MY BEST RECRUITER."

The British recruiting posters from the first year of the war were often presented as a friendly appeal from your pals. One poster stated, 'Why not join the army? You will like it. Your pals will like.' It was about playing the game, which in this case, shown left, was a game of cards. But the war's appetite was insatiable and voluntary service was not enough, and it would finish when the Military Service Bill was passed in January 1916 and came into effect in the spring.

Recruiting poster issued in late 1915 advising men eligible for military service to join voluntarily before the introduction of conscription in the new year. Avoiding 'congestion and inconvenience' does not seem much of an incentive for those who, by this stage, had not already chosen to join up as volunteers.

The quarter deck and some of the crew of HMS *Hampshire*. Note the marines in the foreground, behind the turret.

HMS *Hampshire* at Weymouth prior to the First World War. Note the pinnace at her side, and the men on painters keeping her touched up.

HMS *Oak* was built in 1912 and used almost exclusively at Scapa Flow. During the First World War, she was tender to the flagship of the Grand Fleet and shuttled backwards and forwards from the mainland to Orkney. *Oak* carried Lord Kitchener from Scrabster to Scapa before he transferred to the *Hampshire* for her ill-fated last voyage. HMS *Oak* was used during the surrender of the German fleet to transfer Admiral Meurer to HMS *Queen Elizabeth* to enact the surrender of the German fleet on 15 November 1918, and on the 20th to carry King George V, Queen Mary and the Prince of Wales to see the fleet off the Firth of Forth. She was sold for scrap in May 1921.

*Above and below:* Kitchener, when he died, was still a respected figure for many millions of Britons. The postcard publishers Bamforth, well known for their holiday seaside comic cards, produced a series of In Memorium cards to commemorate Kitchener's death.

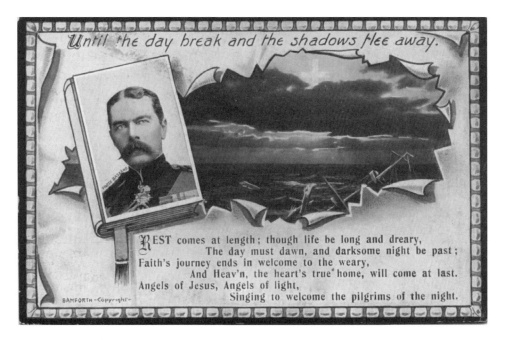

*Above and below:* These two images represent the last ever photographs taken of Kitchener, whose body was never recovered after the sinking of HMS *Hampshire*. The above image shows Kitchener, centre left, about to board the drifter that would take him from HMS *Iron Duke*, where he had had lunch with Admiral Lord Jellicoe, the commander of the Grand Fleet. The image below shows him approaching the wheelhouse of the converted fishing boat. Within hours he would be dead, along with over 600 crew and officers of HMS *Hampshire*.

# KITCHENER'S ARMY

AND THE

# TERRITORIAL FORCES

*The Full Story of a Great Achievement*

BY

EDGAR WALLACE

LONDON: GEORGE NEWNES, LIMITED
SOUTHAMPTON STREET, STRAND, W.C.

# CONTENTS

# INDEX TO ILLUSTRATIONS

# KITCHENER'S ARMY

## AND THE

# TERRITORIAL FORCES

*The Full Story of a Great Achievement*

.BY

## EDGAR WALLACE

### INTRODUCTION

"KITCHENER'S ARMY!"—a phrase which may well stand for a hundred years, and, indeed, may stand for all time as a sign and symbol of British determination to rise to a great occasion and to supply the needs of a great emergency. It is not my task here to discuss the military situation as it might have been, or to offer arguments for or against national service, nor yet to say whether the recruitment of the first few months of the war disposes of or makes inevitable a system of compulsory service. The purpose of this volume is to place on record in a permanent form a chapter of Britain's history of which the people of all ages who call these islands their home may indeed be proud.

The outbreak of war found all the nations concerned unprepared save one. Germany alone, which had been preparing, scheming, and planning for the day on which it would be at war, was ready in every department to the last button on the last service tunic. Germany, with huge reserves of men and stores and warlike material, swept resistlessly down through Belgium and secured for herself a momentary and, as it was thought at the time, an unchallengeable advantage. Russia was not ready, France was not ready, and most certainly Great Britain was not ready to deal with the huge numbers and the great masses which were instantly directed against the Allies.

At the time when the British Army was mobilising in England, and when Russia had no more than 300,000 men on the scene of action, Germany had concentrated forty-four Army Corps, divided into nine Armies,

the smallest of which, under General von Deimling, was charged with the task of keeping strictly on the defensive behind the Vosges. The rest of this enormous mass was concentrated between Aix-la-Chapelle and Strasburg, and the eight Armies which were equipped and in the field days, indeed weeks, in advance of some of the Allies were, reading from right to left (that is to say, from north to south), the first army under von Kluck, the second under von Buelow, the third under von Hausen, the fourth under the Duke of Wurtemburg, the fifth under the Crown Prince of Prussia, the sixth under the Crown Prince of Bavaria, the seventh under von Heeringen, and the eighth army, which was merely temporarily formed, was known as the Army of the Meuse and was under von Emmich.

Von Emmich's Army was immediately ready for service the moment war was declared, and stationed, as it had been before the outbreak, a short distance from the Belgian frontier, it had during the later days of July been brought up to war strength by the secret additions of reserves, who had been personally notified and had been charged to keep their notification to themselves.

The British Army Expeditionary Force, which immediately mobilised on the outbreak of war, was roughly 160,000 officers and men; but only a very small proportion of these was ready for war. When the Germans swept down through Belgium they found themselves opposed at Mons to two Army Corps only (80,000 men), which later,

LORD KITCHENER'S APPEAL FOR RECRUITS MET WITH AN INSTANTANEOUS
RESPONSE FROM HUNDREDS OF THOUSANDS OF BRITAIN'S SONS. THE
PHOTOGRAPH SHOWS THE WHITEHALL RECRUITING DEPOT BESIEGED BY
MEN EAGER TO SERVE THEIR COUNTRY.

BEFORE A RECRUIT CAN BE ACCEPTED HE HAS TO PASS A VERY
THOROUGH MEDICAL EXAMINATION. (PHOTO: *SPORT AND GENERAL*.)

comparative sizes of the armies is instructive.

| Nation. | Peace footing. | War footing. | No. of guns. |
|---|---|---|---|
| Austria . . . | 500,000 | 2,200,000 | 2,500 |
| France (including Algerian troops) | 790,000 | 4,000,000 | 4,200 |
| Great Britain . | 234,000 | 380,000 | 1,000 |
| Germany . . | 850,000 | 6,000,000 | 5,500 |
| Russia . . . | 1,700,000 | 7,000,000 | 6,000 |

As will be seen by the above table, the only advantage—and it was merely a relative advantage—which Great Britain possessed was the larger proportion of guns she had to the number of men under arms, but this advantage is neutralised by the fact that the Indian Native Army, which is not included in this table, possess no guns at all, and depend for their artillery upon the British Army. So whilst at first it seems that we have one gun to every 380 men, if we put in the 200,000 Indian native troops serving, the proportion is reduced to one in 580.

It may be said, and, indeed, has been said, that Great Britain, from the insularity of her position and the protection which her huge Navy and her narrow seas afford her, is not so greatly in need of an Army as was either of her great rivals, who have huge frontier lines to protect and must needs de-

at Le Cateau, were reinforced by a division, and were still further augmented in the early part of September by another Army Corps. Large as was this force from the point of view of a nation which has never engaged more than 160,000 men in any one battle formation since the wars of the Middle Ages, it was insignificant by the side of the great armies which were gathering on the Continent. A little table showing the

pend upon seas of armed humanity to protect their great industrial districts and their strategic positions.

This was largely true; but equally true was it that great armies have functions to fulfil other than the actual winning of battles. It was evident from the beginning that this war could only end when the whole of the map of Europe had been changed, when frontiers had been readjusted and territories acquired or lost by the belligerent Powers, and it was just as evident that, great as might be the influence which a naval Power might exercise in the course of the war, the settlement and the terms of peace would be dictated by the possessors of large land forces. It was evident, too, from the many signs which Germany gave us that she had aimed for many years to secure a world domination, and to impose her will upon the peoples of the earth. Necessarily, Great Britain, of all the countries in the world, stood in the way of her ambitious scheme, and, as inevitably, Germany had planned the overthrow of this country. Britain, however, could only be overthrown by a sequence of circumstances. The first was that she should not intrude herself in this war, but that she should leave Germany and Austria to finish their great antagonists, and establish themselves in Belgium and upon the North Sea, so that at the triumphant end of the war Germany should have a naval base from which she could in course of time operate against her great sea rival. It was evident, therefore, that to make her Navy doubly effective, it was necessary to destroy the enemy's land power.

Events did not turn out as Germany anticipated; and though, by her lightning mobilisation and the rapidity of her march past, she succeeded in obtaining initial successes—and those with great loss—she quickly found her advantages nullified by new and menacing forces which were rapidly coming into existence against her. Undoubtedly the greatest of these forces was the creation in Britain of a most unexpected Army. It denotes the machine-made character of German thought that our enemy did not believe in the existence of that Army, palpable as it was, until he received evidence

RECRUITS TAKING THE OATH AT THE CENTRAL RECRUITING DEPOT, WHITEHALL.
(PHOTO: *SPORT AND GENERAL*.)

RECRUITS ON THEIR WAY FROM THE RECRUITING OFFICES TO THEIR TRAINING CAMPS.

of its excellence and its numbers on the field of battle.

I have related all the circumstances which were responsible for the beginning of Kitchener's Army, and it only remains to add one very important fact, that the reader may appreciate to the full, the extraordinary accomplishment of those entrusted with the conduct of Great Britain's military affairs.

To say that Great Britain was unprepared for this great war is to say that, whilst she was ready to believe that Germany, France,

'H' COMPANY OF THE POST OFFICE RECRUITS MARCHING IN COMPANY FORMATION IN REGENT'S PARK.

Russia, and Austria would some day or other be involved in a world conflict, she did not anticipate that she would be called upon to enter that field, or be asked or expected to organise great military forces to combat Prussian militarism upon land.

She did not, indeed, realise that such a conflict could not be waged without Britain's power and Britain's place amongst the Powers being challenged, not only by one section of the belligerents, but by all.

I have referred to the unreadiness of Great

RAW RECRUITS TRAINING
IN KENNINGTON PARK.
(PHOTO: *CLARKE AND
HYDE.*)

RECRUITS OF THE LINCOLNSHIRE REGIMENT BEING INSTRUCTED IN THE USE OF THE RIFLE. (PHOTO: *SPORT AND GENERAL.*)

Britain to participate in so huge a conflict as that which raged through Europe in the summer and autumn of 1914, and by that I do not mean that our men were ill-trained or ill-equipped. All that is meant is that, while we had the clothing and equipment, arms and ammunition, guns and horses to furnish the British Army and its reserves, we had not supplies for larger forces than the number set down as Britain's normal war strength.

The task the Government set itself was a formidable, nay, a staggering one. It was in the first place to take 500,000 raw men from the streets, from the clubs, from the fields, from the villages, towns, and cities of Great Britain, and not only to train them in the art of war in the shortest space of time that it is possible to train soldiers, but also to prepare the equipment, the arms, and the munitions and stores of war.

And so Kitchener's Army came into existence with a rush. It came into existence in the crowded streets of the great cities, in the peaceful villages up and down England, Scotland, Ireland, and Wales, where men came forth from office, warehouse, and factory, or tramped from their farms and their cottages to the nearest recruiting office; it came into existence on the decks of homeward bound steamers, where little coteries of young men, eager and enthusiastic, returning to their Motherland to give their services, had already joined themselves into parties for enlistment in certain regiments.

## CHAPTER I

### THE MEN OF THE FIRST ARMY.

AN observer watching the animated scene before one of the greatest recruiting centres of London in the early part of August might have witnessed a strange sight—a policeman grasping firmly the arm of a flushed and smiling young man, and leading him gently down the road, past his jeering companions to a point a quarter of a mile from the place whence he had been taken. For this young man had, with great temerity, dared to insinuate himself at the wrong end of the long queue which was waiting its turn to parade before the medical officer and to be examined that its fitness for army service might be certified. This young man could complain, as he did, that he had already been waiting for six hours, that he had journeyed from Canada at the first hint of war, and that he was most anxious to begin working at his new profession as soon as it was possible; but the unanswerable retort was that he was only one of thousands, and that the recruiting authorities were quite unable to cope with the rush of men which had followed the demand of Lord Kitchener and the Prime Minister for the first 100,000 men. The machinery of the peace time recruiting office was not designed to pass thousands of men a day. To pass, as it did, a larger number of recruits for the Army in twenty-four hours than that particular office had passed in a year in normal times was an achievement in itself. In justice to the Chief Recruiting Officer, it cannot be said that his system broke down, but rather that it could not be accelerated beyond a certain speed; and recognising this, the Government established offices, not only in the principal centres of all the great towns of England, but in the outlying suburbs and in the villages and market

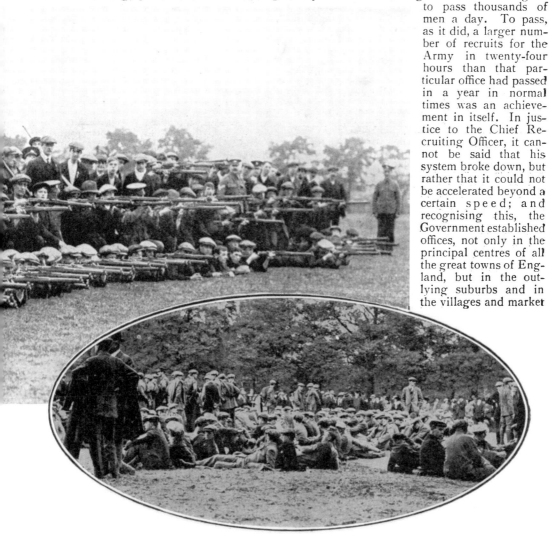

MEN OF THE PUBLIC SCHOOL BOYS' CORPS WAITING TO LEAVE HYDE PARK FOR THEIR CAMP AT EPSOM. (PHOTO: *SPORT AND GENERAL.*)

SWEDISH DRILL IN THE OPEN – THE QUEEN VICTORIA'S RIFLES TRAINING AT HAMPSTEAD.
(PHOTO: *SPORT AND GENERAL.*)

towns which were accessible to would-be recruits. They came in such huge numbers that not only was it impossible to deal expeditiously with them as masses, though the actual examination and swearing-in of individuals proceeded as rapidly as was humanly possible, but it was likewise impossible for a long time to house, clothe, and

ANOTHER EXERCISE OF THE LONDON REGIMENT. QUEEN VICTORIA'S RIFLES, AT HAMPSTEAD.
(PHOTO: *SPORT AND GENERAL.*)

DEVELOPING THE RECRUITS' PHYSIQUE – THE PHOTOGRAPHS SHOW A SQUAD OF FUTURE GYMNASIUM INSTRUCTORS FOR KITCHENER'S ARMY UNDERGOING THEIR TRAINING AT THE GYMNASIUM, ALDERSHOT. (PHOTO: *CLARKE AND HYDE*.)

equip these huge numbers which grew in size every day.

We may imagine our recruit, patiently and cheerfully forming one of the long queue outside the chief recruiting office, shuffling forward at a snail's pace as the queue moved up, and as the men, in parties of six and seven, were released to the medical inspection room, reaching at last the long-desired portal and finding himself ushered brusquely into a large, square apartment, equipped with a weighing machine, a scale for measuring height, a wash-bowl for the medical officer's hands, and two tables, at one of which sat a clerk busily filling up the attestation forms, containing particulars of the recruit's physical appearance, his trade, relatives, and measurements.

In a few moments the would-be recruit is standing erect in nature's uniform. The examination is brief but thorough. Heart and lungs are tested by stethoscope and by judicious tapping. His chest is measured and his exact weight recorded. The recruit hops across the bare room, first on one leg and then on the other.

NON-COMMISSIONED OFFICERS OF THE NEW ARMY UNDERGOING INSTRUCTION IN PHYSICAL TRAINING AT THE HEADQUARTERS' GYMNASIUM, ALDERSHOT. (PHOTO: *GALE AND POLDEN.*)

His teeth are inspected, and then comes the crucial test of eyesight. A small card, containing a number of letters in various types, is placed on the wall opposite him, and he is asked to tell, first with one eye and then with the other, not only the names of the letters indicated, but he is also required to distinguish certain dots, their number, and their formation. A quick examination follows for varicose veins and other infirmities, and then with a curt nod he is dismissed to his clothing. The Medical Officer signs the attestation form, and the recruit is hurried into another room where half-a-dozen men who have also passed the medical officer are waiting their turn.

## "Swearing In."

Presently the recruiting officer enters from his office, accompanied by an orderly, who distributes a number of New Testaments to the waiting recruits, who take them shyly or with that evidence of embarrassment which comes to self-conscious people who are doing unaccustomed things.

"Take the book in your right hand. You swear—say after me, 'I swear.'"

"I swear," repeats the recruit.

"To serve His Majesty the King."

"To serve His Majesty the King," says the recruit, and the oath proceeds—

"His heirs and successors . . . and the generals and officers set over me by His

This was the very beginning. The long, waiting queues the interested lookers-on, the hurry and rush of the recruiting office, the bustle and seeming indifference of the great city—this is the atmosphere in which the first Kitchener soldiers came to the Army. The broad doorway of the chief recruiting office was the gate to a land of strange and tragic adventure and it was with a light heart and a high hope that the young men of Great Britain passed through to the wonderful land beyond.

That was what one witnessed on the Thames Embankment in the heart of London; it was likewise seen in every great town and every small town throughout the kingdom. Birmingham, Manchester, Newcastle, Cardiff—all the great industrial and manufacturing centres, no less than the smaller towns, established or enlarged their recruiting offices and daily sent their quota of new young soldiers to the depôts. I shall have something to say later with reference to the wonderful organisation of these depôts, and the way the rush of recruits was received, sorted out, and distributed over the country to various centres. It was all done on a well-organised plan, on lines in operation in ordinary times of peace. The civilian reader knows little or nothing of these matters. But I hope to make it clear to him what a marvellous achievement

Majesty the King, his heirs and successors, so help me God!"

The book is kissed, and the raw civilian who came into the building on one side goes out at the other a member of the great army which is forming and part and parcel of that brotherhood of arms which "binds the brave of all the earth." He may have asked to be enlisted for some special regiment, and in the beginning, when the War Office called for recruits, it gave a number of friends who cared to come together the privilege of serving together in any regiment they chose, or, if they had no particular choice, in any regiment which the War Office desired to fill.

UNDER COMPETENT INSTRUCTORS KITCHENER'S RECRUITS ARE TAUGHT MANY SPLENDID EXERCISES FOR THE STRENGTHENING OF THE MUSCLES. (PHOTO: *L. N. A.*)

the collection, handling, and distributing of these crowding thousands was in reality. The military authorities had to deal with something they had probably never anticipated in their lifetime. They rose to the greatest emergency in our history.

In the last weeks of August, Mr. Asquith in the House of Commons announced that the Government would ask for credit which would enable the new War Minister, Lord Kitchener, to raise a new army of 500,000 men. This was followed at a later date by the announcement that the first 500,000 would be supplemented by a second half-million. With that announcement began the formation of the Kitchener masses.

One million men ! It was an extraordinary number to the Britisher, who never thought in hundreds of thousands. Men who had

A STRETCHING POSITION IN THE PHYSICAL EXERCISES. (PHOTO: *L. N. A.*)

been discussing this grave and curious matter wherever they met together in railway trains, in the streets, in clubs, in the intervals between the acts at the theatre, asked one another the same question: "Where are we going to get them from?"

The upper and lower middle classes had come to regard the soldier as an individual who was exclusively recruited from certain social strata, just as he regarded wheat as a peculiar and necessary cereal which grew in the fields as a matter of natural course, and with the cultivation of which he himself was not immediately concerned. Volunteering and the Territorial movement he understood, and in this he himself had dabbled, but the Regular Army was apart and aloof from the understanding and from all participation by the thousands of young men occupying

A CORPORAL INSTRUCTS A RECRUIT HOW PROPERLY TO ADJUST HIS PUTTEES.

regular positions in commercial life or entitled to describe themselves as "independent." Certainly these latter never thought of the Army save as an institution to be viewed through the windows of an officers' mess-room. The average young man of Britain was wont to cheer enthusiastically stories of British heroism. He himself was immensely patriotic and honestly desired to serve his country as best he could. That he did not enlist was due not to his lack of patriotism, not to his failure to appreciate the extraordinary demands which were being made upon his country, but just from sheer failure to understand that he himself could be of any service in the ranks of the

WITH THE PUBLIC SCHOOLBOYS AT EPSOM. – LIEUT. F. R. FOSTER, THE FAMOUS CRICKETER, LEADING HIS COMPANY. (PHOTO: *RECORD PRESS*.)

Army. Indeed, it would be fairer to reduce down the preliminary hesitation of the young men of England to a sense of modesty rather than to a desire to shirk.

A few days after the announcement had been made in Parliament that the British Army was to be so enormously increased, there appeared on every public vehicle in London a neat placard to supplement the official posters which at that time were covering the windows of post offices and public buildings and were occupying large spaces in the columns of the daily Press. You saw this appeal in long blue and red

merce—the appeal was working. You could not get away from it. It was flashed upon the screens of picture theatres; it appeared on some of the boards before the theatre doors; it was on the tram tickets; it was pasted on the windows of private houses; it appeared unexpectedly in the pulpit and on the stage; it was printed in neat little characters upon leaflets; it sprawled largely upon the gigantic posters with which private enterprise covered whole facias—"Your King and Country need you."

Young men came up from their homes to

PRACTISING REVOLVER SHOOTING IN THE CRYPT OF
THE KENNINGTON PARISH CHURCH.
(PHOTO: *CLARKE AND HYDE*.)

strips fastened to the wind-screens of taxi-cabs; you saw it on a larger scale plastered to the sides of the motor-buses, so that no men could enter on his journey cityward without receiving an appeal which for a time he honestly regarded as being applied to somebody else !

It took some days for the leaven to work. But in these days the recruiting offices were crowded. A great throng surged into New Scotland Yard; enormously long queues filled with the youth of the City made their way to the recruiting office. One could not walk through a principal street without passing little self-conscious parties being marched down to the nearest railway station to entrain for the depôt of some regiment.

But large as the crowd was, it was, generally speaking, made up of that class of which the rank and file of the Army had aways been formed, with here and there a sprinkling of a better type of man, and although there was no perceptible response to the recruiting literature which was at this time flooding London—that is to say, in so far as it affected the higher grades of com-

their offices, and on the journey they discussed the war, and they expressed their doubt as to whether the number required would ever be raised by voluntary effort. They even went so far as to say that if the worst came to the worst, they would enlist. But in the first few days of the war—indeed, until after the British Army was engaged—the youth of middle-class England took only an academic or enthusiastic interest in the war according to their temperaments, and never conveyed the impression that they themselves were needed in the actual prosecution of the war.

### The Effect of the Great Retreat.

But there came sudden enlightenment, which acted like an electric spark : the retreat from Mons, and the publication of a story in a newspaper which purported to be that of a great disaster to British arms. It was this that stirred the imagination and roused the conscience of our young manhood. It is true that the incident reported was not a disaster, though on first inspection it bore a resemblance to such. But the fact that it was published and that it should have re-

mild exercises of a promenade—and discuss this unbelievable thing, and there was time, too, for the real significance of the news to sink in.

You can only understand the seeming apathy of the nation in the early days of the war (though the superficial observer would see nothing to support the theory of apathy in the huge crowds before the recruiting office) by probing into the British mind, and understanding something of its hopes and beliefs. We had found ourselves allied to two great countries—two great military nations, one of which was capable of putting seven million men in the field,

GETTING FIT FOR THE FRAY – NEW RECRUITS IN THE FIRST STAGES OF MILITARY INSTRUCTION. (PHOTO: *RECORD PRESS.*)

ceived the *cachet* of the Censor, came in the nature of a shock.

This was on a certain Sunday in August. There was one day to think over this terrible news of defeated British soldiers straggling all over the countryside in France; of beaten units, the remnants of what had once been great regiments, coming wearily into the little towns of the north of France, to tell their harrowing story to a shocked correspondent. A whole Sunday in which men could walk up and down the front—for it was summer time and the summer resorts were filled with flannelled young men who found pleasure in the

and the other four million men. We had talked of the Russian "steam-roller" army, which would slowly move across East Prussia, spreading its millions like a cloud of locusts across the fertile lands of Silesia and East Prussia. We knew that the French were so ready for war that on the first trumpet-call three or four million men would stand to arms. But our people knew nothing of the intricacies and the difficulties of mobilisation. They knew nothing of political factors in warfare, that might keep an Army cooling its heels whilst new equipments were procured, or of the enormous distances over which Russian soldiery would have to cross before

RECRUITS BEING TAUGHT THE FIRST MOVEMENTS OF THE BAYONET EXERCISE. (PHOTO: *RECORD PRESS.*)

they could be concentrated on the enemy's front.

On that Sunday there was one question asked: Where are the French? Wherever they were, or whatever they were doing (and we know now how they were occupied), it was obvious they were not in a position at that moment to help this retiring British Army, battling from Mons to Maubeuge, from Maubeuge to Le Cateau, and fighting every inch of its way towards Paris.

That was a thought to ponder on; it gripped them hard.

Monday morning took the great army of young men by train, by 'bus, by tram-car, or driving their own cars in many cases, to their offices and their businesses in the city. At every few yards they were confronted with the simple statement that their King and their Country needed them. Then, perhaps, the inspiration came in a flash that it was *they themselves to whom this appeal was being made*!

Thousands of young men went to their offices on that Monday with their minds made up. The resolution had come. Grave

THE EMPIRE BATTALION OF THE ROYAL FUSILIERS BEING INSPECTED IN GREEN PARK BY MAJOR-GENERAL C. L. WOOLLCOMBE. (PHOTO: *RECORD PRESS.*)

THE LATE FIELD-MARSHAL LORD ROBERTS INSPECTING RECRUITS OF KITCHENER'S SECOND ARMY IN TEMPLE
GARDENS. (PHOTO: *FARRINGDON PHOTO. CO.*)

employers, sitting in their private offices, received deputations in some cases of nine or ten to twenty men, who explained their position. In nearly every case the employer commended, encouraged, and sympathised, and did his part by rapidly improvising a system by which the dependants of his employees should not suffer by the heroism of their men. I know at least one employer who was dumfounded. "Certainly, my young friend," he said to a score of young men who entered his room one after the other to say they meant to offer themselves. "Certainly, my young friend; do so; let me know the result, good luck." These young men went off to the recruiting office *and never returned.* This was what dumfounded their employer. He had the vaguest idea of these things. He expected

ing ground now at a tremendous rate, for it was taking to itself all that was best, physically and mentally, of English manhood.

And now London began to see extraordinary sights. For playgrounds and open spaces, in which the voices of children had predominated, now resounded to the sharp, staccato words of command issued by drill-instructors. The patter of children's feet was gone, and in its place the tramp of marching men. Healthy young Britons in their shirt-sleeves wheeled and formed, advanced and retired, formed two ranks and four at a sharp order, and with head erect and chest expanded, went seriously to the business of preparing themselves for national defence.

The great public parks and open spaces were filled; even in the paved churchyards

RECRUITS OF THE LANCASHIRE REGIMENT CARRYING THEIR BEDS THROUGH A WILTSHIRE VILLAGE TO THEIR CAMP. (PHOTO: *RECORD PRESS.*)

they would all come back and report themselves with a few days allowed them to clear up affairs, enabling him to make fresh arrangements to fill their places! He knows now Kitchener's new men were allowed no days of grace before taking up their training.

New faces appeared in the recruiting queue, a new type of recruit began to elbow its way to the front, first in a trickling stream and then in a whole volume which made the normal river overflow into a dozen little subsidiary streams each making for one of the new emergency recruiting stations which were being opened all over the town. A new tone came to the tents, a new intonation, a suggestion of Public School and University. Kitchener's Army was gain-

of London, one saw these eager recruits at their work. On the sacred lawns of the Inns of Court, whence the pedestrians were warned in time of peace, squads marched and manœuvred. You saw them swinging through the city, alert and cheerful, wearing their civilian garb, without arms, uniform, or equipment, shaking themselves into the mould in which heroes are cast.

Day and night the work went on. Every miniature rifle range was commandeered by the military. New little ranges came into existence in the most unlikely spots. In some cases they were to be found in the gloomy crypts of churches; these offering, as they did, a great amount of quiet space, were utilised to train the men in firing and

A RECRUIT RECEIVING INSTRUCTION IN RIFLE-SHOOTING.

aiming. And even as the recruiting office absorbed its thousands, other thousands came; the congestion grew heavier, though now the streams of recruits moving into barracks had swollen until they were veritable rivers. Half the passengers by the trains which moved out of London north, east, south, and west were men of Kitchener's Army, men who, perhaps, a week before had been sitting in their offices waiting for such news of the war as they could secure from the newspapers, with no idea of themselves forming part of the great brotherhood which was engaged in thrusting back the enemies of civilisation, and who now had a deeper and a more real joy in the knowledge that they were assisting in the great and splendid work.

### What the Employers Did.

Some businesses were wholly denuded of managers, clerks, and employees. But though it might spell ruin to the patriotic employers, no obstacle was placed in the way of men enlisting; and, indeed, the employer realising, perhaps, that he himself was past the military age, prepared a sacrifice on his own part, and offered to the families of these patriots what compensation for the loss of their bread-winners it was possible for him in his circumstances to make.

This enormous influx of recruits was taken to the Army without any sensible disturbance of industry. It was carried out, too, and could only be carried out, with the hearty co-operation and help of the women of England. To the mothers and wives of Kitchener's new Army the nation owes a great tribute of gratitude. No record of the fine achievements which our young men accomplished would be complete unless reference were made to the magnificent spirit of the women of Britain, who sent their men to war without flinching. It was

A SQUAD OF 'A' COMPANY, 8TH BATTALION LEICESTERSHIRE REGIMENT, 'AT THE SLOPE,' AT WOKINGHAM.
(PHOTO: *SPORT AND GENERAL*.)

RECRUITS BUILT THEIR OWN HUTS – CAMBRIDGE UNIVERSITY MEN BUSY WITH THE SAW.
(PHOTO: *SPORT AND GENERAL.*)

on Salisbury Plain; so, also, was Winchester, the great rifle depôts and the headquarters of the Hampshire Regiment; Southampton, where a camp had been established; Devizes, the headquarters of the Wiltshire Regiment, and the great artillery camps at Okehampton might only be reached from this station. Waterloo was, indeed, the military station for all arms, and every train that drew out, whether on its way to Exeter, where the gallant Devons were mobilising, or towards Aldershot, that remarkable soldiers' town, was packed full of light-hearted but determined men, who had already settled down, and had taken to themselves the happy and buoyant spirit of their new profession.

brought about also by the sacrifice of our titled families and of landed proprietors, who not only gave their sons, their money, and themselves to the cause, but placed at the disposal of the military their lands.

All over England, in every private park, on every common, on every recognised camping-ground, were to be seen, in the late summer and the early autumn, the white tents of this new force, and the men themselves, split into squads and companies, were learning the rudiments of their craft near by.

### "The Levelling-up" Process.

Our recruit, with his strange, new friends, who have come so suddenly into his life, but whose faces he will see for many a long day, not only in barrack and camp, but on the field and in the firing trenches before the enemy, marches through this new London, blazing crimson and blue with recruiting posters and cheery appeals to the laggard, to a railway station where hundreds of other small parties are filling the platforms and waiting their turn to shake the dust of London from their feet and begin the serious business of soldiering. Waterloo Station in those days was a remarkable sight. From Waterloo, Aldershot was fed; so, too, was Borden Camp,

Let us picture the position of the new recruit, who has come from a comfortable home, and has had a good education. He is now meeting for the first time, not the soldier confident, alert, and with that indefinable quality which every British soldier possesses of genial tolerance, but new, strange, raw elements, which, perhaps, more than any other, would, in ordinary times, jar on his nerves. He who has come from a house in which his every need has been anticipated, either by a doting parent or by trained servants, finds himself on equal terms with the son of the charwoman, whose existence he had hardly noticed. The son of the charwoman recognises his new comrade, and is the more embarrassed of the two.

What is the logical development of this new mingling of elements? The Army experience teaches us that men in the Army level up, as men in all noble professions must do. Groups having a noble object, or an elevating object, or an object calling

MEN OF 'C' COMPANY, 4TH BATT. ROYAL FUSILIERS, WORKING ON A ROOF.
(PHOTO: *SPORT AND GENERAL*.)

these two will meet together on a common ground, man to man, and find something very admirable in one another, and learn to respect each other's "best."

**The Recruit in Barrack and Camp.**

Let us follow the fortune of the recruit when he has taken the oath of allegiance, and when in company with perhaps fifty or sixty other men, he is marched · through the streets of the town to the railway station which is to carry him to his depôt. He has probably applied for a certain regiment, or, if he has not done so, perhaps a batch of soldiers are required for some particular corps. Since they have no particular wishes in the matter, they are earmarked for the regiment requiring recruits, and in batches

into play all the finest qualities of the race, must, in course of time, reach an average level, a little lower, perhaps, than the highest, but certainly much higher than the lowest, intelligence in that group. This evolution goes on where groups of men are banded for unworthy purposes, but it works exactly the other way about.

It would be absurd to say that instantly, by the mere taking of an oath, these two incompatibles are going to be brought down to a common denominator, if the jumble of · terms be allowed. They will each edge towards one another from the very first. The better-class man will unbend and unstiffen and get down as far as he can ; the other, the more humble, will reach up to the best of his ability. Some day, after hardships mutually endured, after privations commonly shared,

THE FINISHED HUT, THE TEMPORARY HOME OF THE RECRUIT. (PHOTO: *DAILY MIRROR*.)

MEN OF THE KING'S LIVERPOOL REGIMENT AT BAYONET PRACTICE AT
ALDERSHOT. (PHOTO: *RECORD PRESS.*)

of fifty and sixty are marched off to join their unit. Fortunately, when the great rush was on the weather was warm—was, indeed, very hot, and the immediate incon-

veniences which the recruit was called upon to face were not of such a character as to unduly distress him. He arrived at his depôt in some quiet little country town to discover the barracks crowded out, every available

NO. 13 PLATOON, 'D' COMPANY, 5TH CAMERON HIGHLANDERS. (PHOTO: GALE AND POLDEN.)

INNS OF COURT O.T.C. INFANTRY BEING INSTRUCTED IN SLOW MARCHING IN LINCOLN'S INN FIELDS.
(PHOTO: *SPORT AND GENERAL.*)

tent filled, the recreation rooms, libraries, and gymnasiums crowded with men; and he learned with dismay that there was no place for him to lay his head. A somewhat discouraging experience for the young patriot, fired with a desire to serve his country, but one which was borne with infinite good humour. A couple of blankets were handed to him, and he was told to sleep where he could. The weather, as I say, was of such a character that al fresco "lodgings" entailed no great hardship; and under the old trees of the barrack square, or on the sloping meadows behind the barracks, the new-comer laid himself down and made himself as comfortable as he could, enjoy-

ing, perhaps for the first time in his life, a night under the stars.

But all the time the authorities were working at top speed to relieve the congestion. The depôt, crowded as it was, did not hold the newcomer for very long. The skeleton of the new battalion appeared upon some far-away down; a dozen great army transports dumped their canvas bags, their sacks of tent-poles and their floor-boards, and left them in charge of an Army Service Corps officer. Presently appeared an advance party of old soldiers, generally drawn, as far as was possible, from the regular regiments, and, failing those, from the Special Reserves which had had experience of

THE NEW ARMY IN THE MAKING AT ALDERSHOT. (PHOTO: *RECORD PRESS.*)

camping out; and two long lines of white tents appeared, a great marquee for officers' mess, other marquees for stores. A quarter-master arrived on the spot, a small group of officers who surveyed the empty tents a little gloomily, a handful of non-commissioned officers, who drew from the big marquee store—now becoming rapidly furnished with the stationery which is indispensable to army organisation—their various "requisitions" and "returns," their books and their camp equipment. New lorries appeared, long trains of Army Service Corps wagons, filled with blankets, waterproof sheets, arms and ammunition; and then on top of these a few men, obviously old soldiers, chosen for the work, who were quickly promoted to the rank of Lance-Corporal or Corporal, and whose duty it was to find the first guard for the new camp.

And then the men began straggling in. They came in little parties of fifty and a hundred from the depôt, which had fitted them with khaki, carrying their white canvas kit-bags containing spare uniform, boots, shirts, and such knick-knacks and extras as wisdom dictated. Some of them could cook; these were requisitioned at once by the Sergeant master-cook, on the look-out for likely regimental chefs. A great many, perhaps, in the early days could keep accounts; the quartermaster required some of these, the Commanding Officer others. The sprinkling of officers, keeping a sharp look-out for men of intelligence were not slow to distribute chevrons of promotion as the days went by. To the keen man in Kitchener's Army promotion came quickly.

### The Steady Flow of Recruits.

Steadily men were coming in; every evening brought a fresh party, every morning found another line of tents extending farther back from the original line; and every day the gathering of troops upon the adjacent improvised parade-ground grew larger, until upon one fine morning four strong double companies stood to attention, and it was whispered abroad that the battalion was "full."

All this time new officers had been arriving. In some cases they had travelled thousands of miles in order to lend a hand in constructing the Kitchener corps. In one case an officer travelled day and night for 4,500 miles, leaving his ranch—he was farming at the foot of the Rocky Mountains—in order to offer himself as a subaltern. He had been an officer and had retired, and now, at the first call of duty, he had returned, as thousands of others had returned, to the colours.

The battalion was indeed full, and had been full long before the men of that battalion had suspected it. For in another part of the country, and upon yet another open plain, the same process of building had been going on, with the help of men drawn in some cases from the first new battalion. New stores had been erected, new tent lines laid down, and new stragglers had appeared, and by the time the 1st Service Battalion had reached its full complement of men the second was half filled.

So this process went on. One battalion followed hard upon the heels of the other. On different ground, under different conditions, but bound together by the regimental badge they so proudly wore, the young battalion were getting fit.

It will be as well to describe something of the machinery for receiving and distributing the supply of recruits which comes in ordinary times, and which was utilised to such excellent

HIS MAJESTY THE KING, ACCOMPANIED BY LORD KITCHENER, REVIEWING RECRUITS AT ALDERSHOT. (PHOTO: *SPORT AND GENERAL*.)

## THE START OF LORD KITCHENER'S ARMY.

THE FIRST ADVERTISEMENT ISSUED BY THE WAR OFFICE, AUGUST 8TH, 1914.

# Your King and Country Need You.

# A CALL TO ARMS.

An addition of 100,000 men to his Majesty's Regular Army is immediately necessary in the present grave National Emergency.

Lord Kitchener is confident that this appeal will be at once responded to by all those who have the safety of our Empire at heart.

## TERMS OF SERVICE.

General Service for a period of 3 years or until the war is concluded.

Age of Enlistment between 19 and 30.

## HOW TO JOIN.

Full information can be obtained at any Post Office in the Kingdom or at any Military depot.

# GOD SAVE THE KING!

purpose to dispose of the great rush of new soldiers after the outbreak of war and the issue of Lord Kitchener's call.

The United Kingdom and Ireland are divided into a number of "commands." Taking them alphabetically, we come first to the Aldershot command, which includes a part of Hampshire and that portion of Surrey in which the Royal Flying Corps are stationed, at Brooklands. The Eastern command comprises Northamptonshire, Cambridgeshire, Norfolk, Suffolk, Essex, Huntingdonshire, Bedfordshire, Hertfordshire, Middlesex, Kent, Surrey, Sussex, and Woolwich. The Irish command takes in the whole of the troops in Ireland; the London (district) command includes the county of London and Windsor; the Northern command takes in Northumberland, Durham, Yorkshire, Lincolnshire, Nottinghamshire, Derbyshire, Staffordshire, Leicestershire, and Rutland. Then there is the Scottish command. Warwickshire, Worcestershire, Gloucestershire, Oxfordshire, Buckinghamshire, Berkshire, Cornwall, Devonshire, Somersetshire, Dorsetshire, Wiltshire, and Hampshire are in the Southern command. The Western command takes in Wales and the counties of Cheshire, Shropshire, Herefordshire, Monmouthshire, Lancashire, Cumberland, Westmorland, and the Isle of Man.

In these commands the organisation was completed for the creation of three new armies, a number afterwards increased to six, and even then adaptable to increase. These were the armies to be fed through the gaping doors of the various recruiting centres, and it was left to the depôts to make the first rough organisation of the fresh armies and to act as sorting boxes into which the new men were grouped.

In Great Britain and Ireland there are sixty-eight infantry depôts, each designated with a number and generally referred to as the centre of a regimental district. These regimental districts take their numbers from a regiment which has its headquarters at the particular depôt. Thus, the 1st Royal Scots (1st Regiment of Foot) is in Regimental District No. 1; the Queen's 2nd Royal West Surrey Regiment is

will more easily understand how Kitchener's Army came into the forces. We will take the 50th Regiment, the Royal West Kents, with its headquarters and regimental depôt at Maidstone. The 1st and the 2nd Battalions being regulars, the one with the Expeditionary Force and the other in India, we need not trouble about them. The 3rd Battalion was the Reserve battalion. That is to say, it was made up of militia, and, though primarily designed for home defence, could serve in case of emergency as the feeder to the Battalion at the

THE FORTUNE OF WAR – THE LONDON OFFICES OF THE HAMBURG-AMERIKA LINE TRANSFORMED INTO A BRITISH RECRUITING OFFICE. (*G.P.U.*)

in Regimental District No. 2; and so on.

In addition to these sixty-eight regimental depôts, which are the homes of the corps, and in which most of the records are kept, there is a Guards' depôt at Caterham, and a rifle depôt at Winchester—the Rifle Brigade being the one regiment in the British Army which does not boast of a number.

It was on this foundation that the new army began to build. If we take as an example one particular regiment, the reader

Front, or, if necessary, could be employed *en bloc* in the field. The 4th Battalion you will find in the Army list marked with a small circle and a St. Andrew's cross. This is an indication that this battalion, which is Territorial, has volunteered and has been accepted for foreign service. The same mark is found against the 5th Battalion, and, as a matter of fact, both 4th and 5th are employed, and have been sent abroad in order to relieve first line troops which were sent from this country.

After the 5th, in normal times, we might find a record of a Cadets Battalion, but in time of war the Cadet units are dismissed in three short lines. Following the 5th we reach the 6th Battalion, and now we have come to the first of the new "Kitchener" battalions which have enlisted since the war.

After this follow the 7th Service Battalion, and then the 8th and the 9th. This regiment may be taken as a microcosm of the whole army. We have the two regular battalions, one of which is serving in India and one at the Front; we have the Special Reserve, which is probably in England and is being utilised either for home defence or to feed the 1st Battalion; we have the two Territorial battalions, that is to say, the volunteer corps, which have been mobilised and sent abroad in order to relieve first line troops; and we have four brand new regular battalions of that regiment, formed from the men who had taken their place in the queues at the recruiting offices to form part of the new and splendid force which had come forward at the nation's call.

Not all the regular infantry regiments stationed abroad returned, though in the majority of cases they were brought back to the field. But it is safe to say, so far as Kitchener's Army was concerned, that the first results of recruiting meant that, where one man stood in the field at the beginning of the war, he was reinforced by four others before the war had progressed very far.

How did the recruits to Kitchener's Army "shape"? In what manner did the recruit come to his own, and, from being a raw and awkward civilian, slow to move and slower to obey, develop into the smart, alert soldier? The story of his initial hardships and difficulties, of his extraordinary development, of the tragic comedy of his blunders, and of the gradual transformation which came to him, which developed him from an irresponsible civilian into a disciplined soldier of the King, will be told in the next chapter.

KITCHENER'S ARMY HAS HAD NOTHING TO COMPLAIN ABOUT IN THE MATTER OF RATIONS; THE ABOVE IS A TYPICALLY HAPPY GROUP AT DINNER-TIME. (PHOTO: *RECORD PRESS.*)

MEN OF THE SOUTH MIDLAND BRIGADE TAKING A WELCOME REST ON A MARCH.

## CHAPTER II.

### THE RECRUIT'S FIRST DAYS IN THE NEW ARMY.

THE recruit passed from the depôt in a very short space of time, to the battalion to which he was to be attached for the remainder of his service. As a rule three days sufficed to fit him with his suit of blue serge, to be replaced later by khaki, his boots, underwear, and overcoat.

Barrack accommodation was quite inadequate to dispose of the new battalions—the more so since most of the permanent buildings, barrack rooms, &c., were requisitioned by the quartermaster for the safe storing of clothing and equipment. The buildings, therefore, were replaced by tent lines, and where these were insufficient, the remainder of the troops were billeted. In other words, the householders in a town or village were asked to provide sleeping accommodation for the men of Kitchener's Army, and were rewarded at the rate of ninepence per man per diem. For this they were asked to do no more than give him a place to sleep in, and allow him the use of their fire for cooking purposes. Our recruit might, and often did, find himself fallen upon pleasant places. There were pleasant stories of billeting landlords and landladies who provided Private

Brown with his cup of tea in bed, and gave this lucky soldier the liberty of a warm bathroom at all hours of the day and night. The legends which surrounded the billets are numerous. There is the case of a fortunate soldier who journeyed to parade every morning in a most expensive motor-car, and was whirled home, when the parades were finished at night, in the same lordly conveyance—provided by his host.

The average recruit was not so favoured, and upon his arrival with his new battalion, had to be content with tent accommodation. The method of "telling off" was simplicity itself. Upon arrival he and his fellows were formed up for inspection by the adjutant, and so many of the new men were allocated to one company and so many to another. It was then left to the company sergeant-majors to dispose of the newcomers according to the accommodation available.

A great number of huts had to be hurriedly erected to accommodate the troops, more especially after the advent of almost the wettest winter on record. The canvas tent in many places had to be abandoned in favour of the wooden hut. Soon

KIT INSPECTION OF A KITCHENER'S ARMY UNIT AT CAMBRIDGE.

we had "Hut Towns" dotting the landscape all over the country. As an instance of how the welfare of the men was looked after the following story of Lord Kitchener is told. There had been complaints of faulty huts which had been too hurriedly built. He made a surprise visit to a certain camp, examined every completed hut; there were roofs which were not watertight, floors which were imperfect, and so on. Kitchener acted with characteristic promptitude, he would brook no imperilling of the health of the men. He instructed the commanding officer to find billets for the whole of the men at once, and they were not allowed to spend another night in the huts.

Under the guidance of a corporal the new recruit was introduced to his future comrades. The round bell tents, with their curtains rolled up to allow free ventilation, with their blankets neatly strapped at frequent intervals in the circle, were inviting enough, though the recruit could tell that he would find the boards which formed the floor of the tent rather a poor substitute for the mattress he had known in his civilian days.

### The First Night Under Canvas

It was a restless night for the recruit, this first night under canvas in such strange conditions; a night, moreover, in which he realised the limitations of the human frame as he endured the discomforts of sleeping on a wooden floor; in fitful fluttering dozes the night passed. It was almost a relief when the long, trembling call of the

réveille blared through the tent lines, proclaiming the beginning of his day.

He went out into the raw morning air, and was astonished to find, even in the late summer, a white frost on the ground, and to discover also that the water which was brought to the camp by iron pipes from the nearest supply was very cold.

A quick wash and brisk rubbing with his hard towel, and life took on a new and cheerful interest. He was consumed with curiosity as to what the coming day would hold. He remarked with awe and admiration the facility and ease with which the men of the regiment—many of them only his seniors by a few days—fell into the somewhat complicated routine of military service.

Comforted by a cup of coffee, which he ladled from the steaming dixies which the cook had prepared, he fell in to his first parade. By companies the regiment swung through the country lanes at a brisk march, varied now and again by a "double" (that is to say, a jog trot), and after this exhilarating little walk, lasting no more than half an hour, the companies came back to camp to eat a hurried breakfast, and to prepare for the more important work of the day.

As yet he was very ignorant as to rank, and very dubious as to whether the youthful officer who came round in the morning to see that the tent flies were rolled up and that the blankets were neatly folded in tidy heaps was a colonel or a sergeant-major. His stay in the depôt had been a very brief one, a very crowded and somewhat chaotic experience, in the course of which he had neither the time nor the opportunity to acquire even a rudimentary military knowledge. But it was never long before the inquiring recruit found a guide, philosopher and

1ST BATTALION OF CITY OF LONDON TERRITORIALS AT SWEDISH DRILL ON TATTENHAM CORNER PLATFORM.

friend. Searching helplessly round, and most anxious in his strange position to find some new acquaintance, he would come upon the inevitable old soldier who, from the height of seven years' service, would look down with a forbearing eye upon the struggling ignoramus, and, whenever possible, would lend a helping hand.

MEN OF THE 17TH WELSH BATTALION – OTHERWISE KNOWN AS 'THE RHONDA BANTAMS' OR THE 'WELSH GURKHAS' – WITH THE ARMY BOOTS WHICH HAVE JUST BEEN SERVED OUT TO THEM.

One day I heard him patiently explaining.

"That man there with one star on his cuff is a second lieutenant. He's as raw to

WHEN LORD KITCHENER INSPECTED MANY THOUSAND TERRITORIALS ON EPSOM DOWNS THE WEATHER WAS WINTRY IN THE EXTREME, BUT NEVERTHELESS THE MEN LOOKED VERY CHEERY AND FIT AS THEY MARCHED TO THE PARADE GROUND.

you, because he doesn't know anything. If you want any advice come to me."

An astounding and arrogant claim, but perfectly justified, as the recruit was to discover.

"The other chap over there with one stripe on his arm— we call it a 'dog's leg' because of its shape—is a lance-corporal. The man

the game as you are, but he's learning. Don't take much notice of what he tells with two stripes is a stripes, a sergeant. corporal; with three The man with the

CAMBRIDGE HAS BEEN 'OCCUPIED' BY KITCHENER'S ARMY, AND SEVERAL OF THE COLLEGES HAVE BEEN FULL OF SOLDIERS. THE PHOTOGRAPH SHOWS TRINITY COLLEGE IN THE HANDS OF THE MILITARY.

crown above his three stripes is the old colour-serjeant. We call him company sergeant-major now, but he's just about the same as ever."

This the recruit learnt at breakfast-time; a breakfast which was surprisingly luxurious, consisting of tea, bread and butter, eggs, and just enough bacon to give flavour. This breakfast had come mysteriously from nowhere. Later he was to discover that at the far end of the camp things had been moving since before réveille, and whilst the

battalion had been doing its little constitutional, there had been great breakings of eggs and splutterings of frying bacon, whilst steaming kettles had been bubbling over their wood fires, and the restless cooks had been working at top speed to provide a thousand hungry men with their breakfast.

Breakfast had hardly finished when the warning bugle sounded, and the tent orderly —he whose duty it was to draw rations and to clean up the tents—had only begun his squad. It was not called the "awkward squad"; it bore the more euphonious title of the "recruits' first squad"; it included a surprising number of men who, unlike himself, perhaps, were not quite clear that their "rights" differed materially from their "lefts," but who, like himself, were anxious to be initiated into the mysteries, even if they did confuse their right foot with their left at times.

### Beginning to Learn

Let us start at the beginning of the training. It was a business full of startling discoveries for the new Kitchener men. The recruit was taught the first position of a soldier, which, so far from being a matter of simple understanding, required very serious effort "Body erect, head up, feet turned out at an angle of forty-five degrees, chest out, shoulders back, arms hanging loosely to the sides with the hands lightly clenched a little behind the seam of the trousers." No, it was not simple. When he was asked to extend his chest, he protruded too much of that part of his anatomy which lies due south of the chest. In other words, he had a disposition to force into prominence that portion of his body upon which, according to Napoleon, the Army marches, but which in practice affords the greatest trouble, not to the commissariat department of the Army, but to the drill instructor.

It was a strained and awkward position in which he found himself. He had been accustomed to allow his shoulders to slack forward. He had developed on his back the

work when the blue-coated figures fell in again in four long lines to answer their names and to undergo the trial of an inspection.

Our new recruit at first was painfully conscious of his awkwardness; how awkward he was he did not realise until he found himself in the unenviable position of right hand man of the awkward

A RECRUIT BEING TAUGHT THE REGULATION SALUTE.

suspicion of a hump, which in the Army is called "the boy." This phrase was a perplexing mystery to the recruit, and when he was placidly requested by the exasperated sergeant to "take the boy off his back," he looked round puzzled and bewildered. When the nature of the request had begun dimly to sink into his mind, when he came to realise that standing erect in the first position of a soldier was something of an achievement, the sergeant proceeded to explain other mysteries.

For instance, when a soldier turns with his whole body, he does so upon scientific principles. The recruit, who had managed for many years to turn to the right or to the left regardless of any scientific rules on the subject, showed a not unnatural desire to dispense with the instructions imparted to him in making this movement. He

BODY BENT SIDEWAYS AND LEG RAISED – ONE OF THE
EXERCISES OUR RECRUITS HAVE TO PERFORM.

was considerably surprised to discover how awkward he looked and felt when he shuffled to his appointed place, generally a few seconds after the remainder of the squad, who had already mastered the intricacies of the movement. He learned that, to turn right about, both knees had to be kept straight and the body erect while he swung round on the right heel and left toe, the left heel and right toe being raised. Then when the right foot was flat on the ground, the left heel had to be brought smartly up to the right, and brought into proper position without being stamped on the ground.

All this was very interesting to me as I looked on; it was equally interesting to watch the sergeant or corporal in charge

A STRONG DORSAL EXERCISE – FORWARD LYING, TRUNK BENT FORWARD,
ARMS STRETCHED UPWARDS.

of the squad showing the "young ideas" how they were expected to show respect and deference to superiors in a perfectly mechanical yet picturesque style — in other words, how to salute. Possibly the instructor did not trouble to explain that when

SWEDISH EXERCISES. AT THE WALL-BARS – LEG-RAISING.

the soldier raises his hand to the salute he is merely carrying out the practice of the knights of old, who, as they rode in the lists past the enthroned queen of beauty, raised their hand politely, that their eyes might not be dazzled with her splendour. That, at any rate, was the beginning of the military salute, whether the sergeant explained it or whether he did not.

"Saluting isn't as easy as it looks," remarked the man who knew. "You must swing your arm up stiffly in a line with your body, your elbows on a level with your shoulder; then you must smartly bend the arm and bring your palm to the head, so that the fingers of your hand rest an inch above your right eyebrow. Many recruits tried other ways of saluting, I noticed. One would bring his hand forward so that his

2ND LIEUTENANT CYRIL ASQUITH, A SON OF THE PRIME MINISTER, DRILLING WITH THE QUEEN'S WESTMINSTERS ON HAMSTEAD HEATH.

CLIMBING THE INCLINED ROPE – A DIFFICULT EXERCISE.

'HANDS UP!' – BUT NEVER TO THE GERMANS! RECRUITS AT A PHYSICAL DRILL WHICH WILL BRING THEM TO FIGHTING FITNESS.

SITTING ON NOTHING IS NOT SO EASY AS IT MIGHT APPEAR.

THE GYMNASTIC FEAT OF 'DOWNWARD CIRCLING' IS ONE THAT OUR SOLDIERS HAVE TO LEARN.

THE LIGHTER SIDE OF SOLDIERING. THE CITY OF LONDON FUSILIERS ASSIST A COMRADE TO TAKE A BATH.

palm blotted out his nose. Invited to try again, he would touch his hat like an ostler. There was only one proper way, however, and he was hectored into it; after a painful ten minutes, the recruit was at last saluting mythical officers with great gravity and earnestness. He had at last come to the conclusion that he would receive no en-

AFTER THE DOCTOR'S VISIT – WELSH SOLDIERS WHO HAVE BEEN INOCULATED AGAINST TYPHOID.

couragement from the instructor in any attempt to introduce into the British Army a novel way of saluting.

Brief as the time had been at the recruit's disposal since he rose that morning, he had been expected to do something which he hadn't done. This he discovered on the after-breakfast parade.

"Take that man's name, Sergeant," said the officer commanding the company; and the recruit indicated learnt that he was delinquent in some respect. Soon, to his shame, he was to learn wherein he had failed. A better-informed comrade on his right supplied him with the information.

the ranks, confessing your shame to the world, readjust the deficiency, and step forward again into the level ranks which offers a comforting haven to you once more.

Nevertheless, the recruit in his desperation must make further inquiries.

"What will happen to me?" he asked in a whisper.

The old comrade, staring blankly to the front, and speaking without moving his lips, supplied the information.

"You'll have to parade at réveille to-morrow morning fully shaved, which means you'll have to get up half-an-hour before anybody else, my lad. And you have to

RECRUITS HAVE THEIR FEET INSPECTED AFTER A ROUTINE MARCH.

"Not shaved," he muttered under his breath.

"But I only shave every other day," protested the recruit.

A sharp voice silenced him.

"Stop talking in the ranks!"

Apparently you must do nothing in the ranks but stand in the first position of a soldier. You must neither talk nor turn your head, nor shuffle your feet until the order to "stand easy" allows you to do so. If you find that a loose button or an unhooked collar necessitates the movement of your hands, you must step two paces from

shave every day whether you like it or not."

The inspection being over, the recruits were sorted into various squads. To the lowest of all, the recruits' squad, the new man had to make his way. Others farther advanced, and the envy of the battalion, were those already engaged in the noble exercise of bayonet drill; but for the young recruit neither rifle nor bayonet was yet available. His work consisted of a continuous succession of drills which had for their object the strengthening of his frame and the development of his physique.

CAMP BUTCHERS WITH THE SPORTSMAN'S BATTALION (ROYAL FUSILIERS) CUT UP THE MEAT FOR DINNER.

MAKING HIMSELF AT HOME IN A BILLET, A RECRUIT
COOKING HIS DINNER.

The recruit was not handed his rifle forthwith. Even if that were desirable, rifles were as yet too scarce to go round. It is true that toward the end of his awkward squad stage, one rifle, jealously and grudgingly loaned, was placed on a tripod before the squad, an object of veneration, and that one by one the men of the squad were allowed to take "sights" with it, but no more. So his time passed in a day made up of "heels raised . . . head bent . . . right bend . . . left bend . . . neck stretch. . . . What the deuce do you think you are doing, Private Clark, imitating Mr. Blooming Tree as Falstaff? Stick your chest out . . . *that's* not your chest! . . . Now we will try it again for the benefit of Private Clark . . . heels raised . . . head bent. . . ."

Amusing for the squad, but a little trying for Private Clark, who went to bed that night and groaned as he turned his aching form on the unyielding boards.

In three days he would be as much an expert as the best of the squad.

Upon the regimental sergeant-major and the N.C.O.'s fell the principal burden of instruction. "Sergeant What's-his-name" had some better material than the "mud," which Kipling sings of, to work upon, but

MEN OF THE LONDON SCOTTISH AT KINGSBURY RECEIVING RATIONS FROM THE SERGEANTS.

the recruit in his "grub" stage—before he became even a chrysalis—was something of a trial, only to be borne patiently, because of his enthusiasm. "Your right side, Private Smith, is the side you shake hands with," said a long-suffering sergeant to a more than usually obtuse private. "What side do you shake hands with?"

"I never shake hands, Sergeant," said the cheerful recruit. "I always say, 'What ho!'"

### Physical Training

Time passes quickly when one is engaged in congenial occupation. Doubtless with his mind fully occupied with the new knowledge he is acquiring, a young soldier finds on the first morning of his training that the order to "stand easy" arrived much sooner than he expected. That he should not feel the effect of standing still for too long a period—one of the greatest trials, I think, that a recruit endures—the movements were varied by what might appear to the onlooker needless marches up and down the parade ground, in the course of which he learnt how to turn or wheel about whilst on the move. This latter process required less scientific effort, it being merely necessary that he should emphasise the change

CARRYING THE RATIONS FOR DISTRIBUTION.

A CAMP KITCHEN AT ALDERSHOT.

of his direction by a smart stamp of the foot. All this was quite simple compared with the drill which followed later in the day.

In ordinary times the young recruit goes through a course of physical training at the depôt or regimental gymnasium. The minds which improvised the great

A MODEL COOKHOUSE ON THE BELTON PARK ESTATE, GRANTHAM. THE KITCHENS ARE SCRUPULOUSLY CLEAN AND WONDERFULLY EQUIPPED.

Kitchener army did not hesitate at improvising gymnasia.

The course of physical drill was considerably changed, and only at Aldershot, where the large gymnasium offered facilities not so much for the recruit as for future instructors of gymnasia, was the old Army course maintained. The work or drill designed to improve the physique of the soldier was carried out in the open air.

The gymnasium work of a regiment is largely in the hands of the gymnasium sergeant (crossed swords over his three stripes indicates his calling). There were

ing public. Here were admirable ready-made substitutes for the usual parallel bars!

Here Kitchener's men became gymnasts, here they discovered what muscular development entailed. A man with sufficient courage to walk up to the mouth of a cannon would retire baffled and discouraged by reason of flabby muscles and stiff joints because of inability to perform balancing feats on a bar. He would flounder ignominiously on mother earth like an overturned fowl on the roadway; he would pick himself up, try again, and probably land on the crown of his head, to the delight

RECRUITS AT THEIR EARLY MORNING TOILET.

hardly enough of these N.C.O.'s to go round the 390 odd new battalions which came into existence in the first months of the war.

Something less grand, therefore, than the palatial gymnasium at Aldershot had to serve, and something more ready-made than the expensive apparatus and contrivances with which that and other institutions are furnished had to be found. And it was quickly done. A visitor to Blackheath, drawing near to Greenwich Park in those days, would witness a startling and entertaining spectacle. A new use had been found for the bars which, in peaceful times, protect the lawns from the encroach-

of the interested spectators. When he had had as much as the instructor felt was good for him for the time being, he would be moved along elsewhere to undergo more gruelling.

No apparatus this time; he was now to practise bodily contortions. He was invited to bend forward and outwards so that his hands could touch his toes or the ground. He had to follow the movements of his instructor in bending the trunk and neck backwards and forwards and sideways, this way, that way, and the next way, with endless variations and combinations of such-like exercises. Look at the illustrations of these exercises in this work, you men of

THE INTERIOR OF THE SERGEANTS' MESS AT GREY TOWERS, HORNCHURCH.

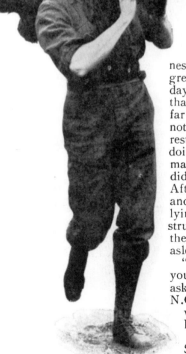

PRIVATE C. ARMSTRONG, A CAMBRIDGE BLUE, CARRYING A USEFUL LOG FOR THE FIRE.

civilian habits who have not joined Kitchener's army, and try what you can do. And this was only a small part in the training to develop the men's physique. The Army instructors mostly aimed at physical drill which could be carried out without any apparatus whatever.

There was running drill, there was the marching, there was (later) bayonet exercise (a fine muscle-developer), trench digging, and so on.

In these early days the men who simply could not master the rudiments of their work from sheer weakness were treated with the greatest of lenience. One day the instructor noticed that a man lying at the far end of the line did not raise his legs as the rest of the squad were doing, and, thinking the man was exhausted, he did not admonish him. After ten minutes passed and the man was still lying on his back, the instructor walked to where the man lay—he was fast asleep.

"Where the dickens do you think you are?" asked the wrathful N.C.O. "Staying a week-end at the Ritz?"

"I was dreaming, Sergeant," replied the apologetic recruit.

"Do you think you'll beat the Germans by

KITCHENER'S MEN AT ALDERSHOT AT LEAP-FROG, AN EXERCISE WHICH FORMS A PART OF THEIR PHYSICAL DRILL.

dreaming?" demanded the exasperated officer.

"That's just what I was dreaming!" replied the recruit triumphantly. "If you hadn't woke me up, the blooming war would have been over!"

It was just about this time, when these methods of developing his bodily fitness became part of his daily life, that the new recruit began to commune with himself on the subject of the exactions the military life made on his physical endurance. Every new experience widens a man's outlook. He began to understand that the erect carriage, the steady step, the perfect balance and bearing of the men of a crack corps, is the outcome of much labour and training.

The very man who, in his civilian days, had taken pride in his supposed strength, and gloried in his elegant physique, was now confronted with humiliating experiences. Compared with the standards of endurance he had now to face, he had to admit to himself that his physical fitness was not so much to boast of after all. Watching his instructor raising himself upon his hands or, stretched on his back, lifting his stiffened legs until his extended toes were pointing to the blue heavens above—and all without any perceptible effort, the learner groaned to

AWAITING THE WORD OF COMMAND – MEN OF THE ROYAL FIELD ARTILLERY READY FOR A TRIAL OF STRENGTH.

IN THE FOOTBALLERS' BATTALION MANY OF THE FIRST-CLASS PLAYERS HAVE ENLISTED, AND THEY ARE AS KEEN ON GETTING FIT FOR THE FIELD OF WAR AS THEY WERE FOR THE FIELD OF PLAY.

think he would have to follow the lead of the instructor to the bitter end.

For the amazing sergeant could go through all this a couple of dozen times. Not so the quaking recruit. After a second or third attempt his poor arms were aching, his legs groggy, and his nerves a bit wobbly. It was an embarrassing revelation to him; he learned for the first time of the lazy muscles which had never been called into play, of idle do-nothings that all his life had evaded their responsibility. In other words, he realised he had muscles in his body which he had never dreamt of. The discovery at first troubled him, and then braced him to further effort, enjoyed with growing relish.

He quickly saw, too, what it was all leading up to—this physical drill, designed not merely to keep the men fit and well, but because it was necessary before a recruit could even begin to become an efficient soldier that his physique should be developed beyond the conditions in which the examining officer found it. It was all arranged to build up the physique necessary for the soldier life. The physical training aimed at the co-ordination of the body and the nervous system; thus only can all-round fitness, muscular development, and stamina be acquired. Mothers and fathers of the young recruits were soon to see for themselves what transformations were effected in their sons by this training by Swedish exercises in the open air, by the severe drilling, and by moral and physical discipline. The change was wonderful. A notable instance was provided by one regiment, every member of which, after a few weeks' training, had to be measured for a new uniform, having completely outgrown the old.

**What other Squads were doing**

Whilst this physical drill was proceeding, a more advanced squad

was elsewhere learning the more interesting part of the soldier's work. The supply of rifles in the early days was quite insufficient to arm the enormous numbers of recruits which were coming in. Some battalions, more fortunate than others, had sufficient rifles, at any rate, for the older recruits.

It was indeed a joyous day when the young soldier was regarded as sufficiently advanced in his profession to be entrusted with a rifle, and fell in upon parade to learn something of this strange instrument which was placed in his hands. He was asked the inevitable question :—

"Why is the rifle placed in the hands of the soldier?" and, after a moment's thought, he answered, as inevitably :—

"To protect my life."

The gorgeous opportunity, seized by successive generations of drill instructors, was once again snapped up.

"Your life," replied the instructor, with fine scorn, "who on earth bothers about your life? The rifle, my lad, is placed in your hands for the destruction of the King's enemies."

And that was the first lesson the recruit was taught, a real lesson of war; the first hint he received of the grim task which was his. There was never a recruit yet who did not carry away from that first instructor's drill a new sense of his responsibility to the State.

The rifle is a strange instrument to handle. There are certain rites and ceremonies associated with its possession and carriage which the recruit had to learn. When for the first time he heard the command "Stand at ease," and then "Stand easy," what was more natural than that he should assume the attitude which, with the pictures beloved of youth still in his mind, he had come to think was not only natural but a little heroic? A watchful sergeant was ready to scorn this attitude. It was one which you may easily visualise.

THE FOOTBALLERS' BATTALION TRAINING AT THE WHITE CITY, LONDON.

The recruit would be standing legs apart, hands one over the other resting on the *muzzle* of the rifle. Now there are many reasons why a soldier should be forbidden to stand in this picturesque position; and in this particular case the reason was that, were the rifle by misadventure loaded, and, by a greater mischance, exploded, the recruit's hands, no less than any other portion of his person which came in the way of the bullet, would be shattered.

The second (to the sergeant the i m p o r t a n t) reason is that the palm of the hand is inclined to perspire, and perspiration, which may get into the muzzle of the rifle, works such havoc as to drive the armoury sergeant mad.

Since the armoury sergeant is responsible for all the arms of the battalion, his point of view is of more consequence really than the view of the medical officer, who might be called upon to patch up all that remained of the too venturesome recruit.

And it is equally forbidden to carry any weight— a bundle or the like—over the shoulder by means of the rifle. For the soldier's salvation, and in the interests of his country, it is necessary that his rifle should at all times shoot straight; any strain upon the barrel of a rifle, even though to the outward eye it should show no sign of bending, is calculated to throw out all the carefully adjusted sights.

"There's another thing you've got to learn," I heard the old comrade explaining to the recruits when the parade had been dismissed; "and that is, you must never fix your bayonet in a barrack-room or in a tent, and you must never point your rifle at anybody under any circumstances."

"Why not, if it isn't loaded?" suggested the recruit.

"Unloaded rifles are always loaded," was the cryptic reply, "and it's a court-martial crime to do any of the things I tell you about. For instance, it is a court-martial

THE PIONEER BATTALION OF KITCHENER'S ARMY (8TH BATTALION OXFORDSHIRE AND

crime to whistle the Dead March in your tent." Death is held in peculiar sanctity in the Army. If the sentry "turns out the guard to all armed parties and to members of the Royal Family" (as his orders run), no less does he turn out the guard, which will stand presenting arms, to the meanest pauper funeral which passes his post.

Such was the elementary work of the recruit in the first days of his training. Very soon he was continually being initiated into new mysteries, and within a very short time after the first response to Lord Kitchener's call to arms, the countryside was alive with whole armies of soldiers in the making.

Parliament had sanctioned an increase of the regular army by two millions. In November it was announced that the figure

BUCKS LIGHT INFANTRY) TRENCH-DIGGING ON THE OUTSKIRTS OF OXFORD.

theatres, skating rinks, cinema halls, winter gardens, and any other available building was commandeered for military purposes; they all echoed to the tramp of these eager feet. It was on a country road where, at a little bridge, which carried the tramping men over a river running at full flood, that I heard the old comrade explaining to a recruit who had asked for the reason of the order to "Break step."

"You mustn't keep step on piers or 'bridges," said he, "because the shock of uniform marching damages the structure even of the strongest bridges, so that if a battalion was crossing Waterloo Bridge in London, the order would be given to 'break step.'"

I travelled the country from east to west and from north to south. Aldershot, Laffan's Plain, and the Sussex Downs were marvellous spectacles. I saw and wondered. I saw the newest recruits labouring at their elementary task, such as I have already sketched. I saw the men as they became more and more advanced, drilling in every department of arms. There were the men in squad and company drill, the men of the machine-gun

of a million had already been reached, and that recruits were coming in at the rate of 30,000 a week. And so it went on. More and more thickly the countryside became populated with men in khaki.

The spectacle of regiments drilling on every suitable training ground, of battalions route marching through town and village, of tents and huts springing up on every side was a glad guarantee of big things to come.

The barrack square was no longer the old time barrack square. It was new ground Kitchener's men improvised for themselves. In field or meadow, on the moors, at the seaside, where the fine firm sands made excellent drill ground—it was there the great work proceeded without ceasing, but with well-ordered and purposeful method. When work had to be carried on indoors,

section, the field engineers, the artillerymen, the cavalry, the motor-cycle corps, the scouts, the signallers, squads at bayonet practice, musketry training, the transport corps, and whole armies route marching or at manœuvres, skirmishing, taking ambush, charging up steep slopes and hills, entrenching, erecting barbed wire defences, and practising every conceivable movement they would have to undertake when the time came in real and deadly earnest to fight in the cause of right and freedom. Here is what Rudyard Kipling wrote of it all; and I endorse what his virile pen has written. One could see how splendidly the men had come on, he said, in a few weeks. "It was a result the meekest might have been proud of, but the New Army does not cultivate useless emotions. Their officers and their instruc-

LEARNING THE ART OF TRENCH-DIGGING – A SQUAD OF 'A' COMPANY, 8TH (SERVICE) BATTALION LEICESTERSHIRE REGIMENT AT WORK.

SINCE THE OUTBREAK OF WAR THE LONDON PARKS HAVE BEEN EXTENSIVELY UTILISED FOR DRILLING BRITAIN'S NEW ARMY.

tors worked over them patiently and coldly and repeatedly, with their souls in the job: and with their soul, mind, and body in the same job the men took—soaked up—the instruction. And that seems to be the note of the New Army.

"They have joined for good reason. For that reason they sleep uncomplainingly double thick on barrack floors, or lie like herrings in the tents and sing hymns and other things when they are flooded out. They walk and dig half the day or all the night as required; they wear—though they will not eat—anything that is issued to

them; they make themselves an organised and kindly life out of a few acres of dirt and a little canvas; they keep their edge and anneal their discipline under conditions that would depress a fox-terrier and disorganise a champion football team. They ask nothing in return save work and equipment. And being what they are, they thoroughly and unfeignedly enjoy what they are doing; and they purpose to do much more."

The work went on from early morning to late at night. There was the morning parade round the town or through the country lanes before breakfast; there was

## BADGES OF RANK: HOW TO DISTINGUISH BRITISH OFFICERS.

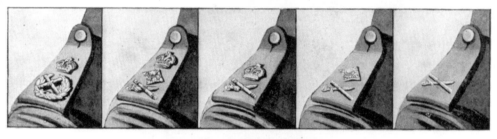

### ON THE SHOULDER STRAP

| Crossed batons on a wreath of laurel with a crown above indicate | Crossed sword and baton with a crown and star above indicate | Crossed sword and baton with a crown above indicate | Crossed sword and baton with a star above indicate | Crossed sword and baton alone indicate |
|---|---|---|---|---|
| **A Field-Marshal** | **A General** | **A Lieut.-General** | **A Major-General** | **A Brigadier-General** |

### ON CUFFS

| A crown and two stars indicate | A crown and one star indicate | A crown alone indicates | Three stars indicate | Two stars indicate | One star only indicates |
|---|---|---|---|---|---|
| **A Colonel** | **A Lieut.-Colonel** | **A Major** | **A Captain** | **A Lieutenant** | **A Second Lieutenant** |

### ON THE ARM (NON-COMMISSIONED OFFICERS)

| A crown, crossed swords, bugles, and three stripes, indicate | A crown, crossed flags, and three stripes, indicate | A crown and three stripes indicate | Three stripes indicate | Two stripes indicate | One stripe indicates |
|---|---|---|---|---|---|
| **Colour-Sergeant** (Rifle Regiment) | **Colour-Sergeant** | **Company Sergeant-Major** | **Sergeant** | **Corporal** | **Lance-Corporal** |

| 4 Sections = 1 Platoon. 4 Platoons = 1 Company | | | | |
|---|---|---|---|---|
| 1 Section —<br>2 Section —<br>3 Section —<br>4 Section — | PLATOON | PLATOON | PLATOON | PLATOON |

A Company about 260 men

DIAGRAM SHOWING SECTION COMPOSITION OF A COMPANY.

half-an-hour for this meal, then every man to his job until a little after midday, with an hour for dinner. From two until half-past four further drills, marches, or manœuvres, with the briefest of rests. Between four and five came tea; and even then for most of the men the day's work was not done.

They were for ever learning, these Kitchener soldiers, with precious little time or inclination for play. The evenings would often be taken advantage of by conscientious company officers, who, if there were no night operations to perform, would lecture the soldiers upon war and its practice. Very often the company officer had himself been attached to some regiment at the front, thus seeing war conditions and acquiring knowledge which was of immense value to him and no less valuable to the recruit. I listened to many a catechism of an old soldier by inquiring recruits, and the man who knew was quick and willing to befriend these eager listeners.

"When do they teach us," asked a recruit of him, "how to tell one officer from another?"

It was a question that staggered his unofficial instructor, but after casting his mind around helplessly, as though for some dim memory of such a course of training, he had to admit that none was ever given, in his recollection.

"Second-lieutenants have one star on their cuffs, and on the shoulder-strap of their overcoats, lieutenants have two, captains three. A major has a crown, which is different from the sergeant-major's crown, because the major's is worked in worsted. A lieutenant-colonel has a crown and star. A colonel has two stars and a crown."

PRACTISING SHOOTING AT THE MINIATURE RANGE AT THE SCHOOL OF MUSKETRY.

"What about a general?" asked the recruit, and the old soldier smiled.

"You'll never be close enough to a general to need worry about that," he said, and went into a long explanation of crossed swords and batons, stars, and crowns.

"Some of the officers have little pieces of red cloth on their collar," said another. "Who are they?"

"You needn't bother about those either," said the old soldier. "They're officers on the staff. That is to say, they're not connected with regiments, but assist the General in his administration."

It was very difficult for the recruit to distinguish officers of one regiment from another. It is true they had badges on each lapel of their tunic, but these were in dull bronze and almost indistinguishable. The doctor he came to know by the little round circle containing the snake of Æsculapius twisted about a staff. The chaplain he recognised by the black Maltese cross he wore on his lapels. But the officers of other regiments who came and went in the great camp were mysteries to him—unsolved until a much later period in his career, when he came to realise what badges represented, and how certain symbols stood for a peculiar kind of regiment.

The old soldier was very informative on these matters.

"All Fusilier regiments have a little bomb with a burst of flame in brass on their collars," he said. "All Light Infantry regiments have a bugle in their badge, and all regiments raised in India before the Mutiny have a tiger."

And so the inquiring mind was satisfied bit by bit.

In reality the evening meal was the first

## SOME INFANTRY BUGLE CALLS

Retreat.

breathing space the Kitchener soldier had since réveille. It was a very good meal, consisting of tea, bread and butter and jam, with an occasional relish. It was, too, the last official meal of the day. For some extraordinary reason the Government has never recognised the need of a soldier in respect to a supper, except in so far as it has christened the 4.30 repast by that name!

Between half-past four and half-past seven the following morning no meals were officially prepared, and the young soldier had to depend upon the coffee and food of every description which he could purchase at the regimental canteen.

There was one point on which he was considerably puzzled; and here again the Army provided no mentor for him other than his chance-met comrade. Every quarter of an hour, when off parade, and very frequently when he was on parade, he heard bugles sounding, and at first there was very little to assist him to distinguish one call from another.

"There are a few you ought to know," said the old comrade. "You need not worry about the réveille, because you'll be asleep through one-half of it and only half-awake through the other. The first call a soldier learns is the 'cook-house' for meals. The easiest one to remember is 'Lights out,' which is a single blast. The only ones that affect you by yourself whilst you're a private are the 'alarm,' the 'assembly,' and the 'fire call.' There are no field calls now, all the orders being given by whistles and signals."

The recruit had therefore to pick up the calls as best he could. During the leisure hour which tea-time brought to him, he might hear one of the most beautiful of the calls—the "Retreat" (a call which marks the end of the day, and not the retirement of troops, as might at first appear)—and most recruits date their beginning of knowledge, so far as the bugle is concerned, from learning this tune.

The origin of the traditional words fitted

to the music by the soldiers is lost in antiquity. Tommy, always humorous, has invented burlesque renderings of them that were far more to his liking than the authorised words. These unauthorised jingles were often unflattering, but always amusing and effective.

Thus Tommy has parodied the Officers' Mess call in these lines : —

Officers' wives have puddens and pies,
Soldiers' wives have skilly—
The jolly old cook he fell in the fire,
And never got out till réveille.

while this was his rendering of the joyful "Dismiss—No Parade" call : —

Oh, there's no parade to-day,
There's no parade to-day,
The colonel has a stomach-ache,
The adjutant's away.

His version of the meals, or "cook-house" call, was distinctly unfair, and is most cer-

tainly not true to-day, when no fault can be found with the generous way Tommy is fed : —

Go for the rations
Orderly man,
Stale bread and meat
And mouldy old jam.

The period which followed tea was not always free for the recruit. There was either a lecture or a night march of some kind to be carried out, and it was not until about half-past seven that he was finally dismissed, either to amuse himself in the recreation rooms which private generosity gave, or the Government provided, or else to seek repose for his weary body in the shelter of his tent.

The latter course was the more appealing to thousands, who found in the early days of their service that seven-thirty left them little more than sufficient energy to drag themselves to the regimental coffee room, where, after the lightest of suppers, they

THE 'EXECUTION' OF A 'SPY' AT ST ALBANS.

MEN OF THE 70TH INFANTRY BRIGADE, IN TRAINING AT FRENSHAM PARK, HAVING DINNER IN A BIG MARQUEE.

returned to find rest on the floor-boards of the tent.

Bed-making was a simple process. Where mattresses were provided, the recruit had to unroll his bedding, spread the blankets, undress and utilise his clothing as a bolster, get in between the blankets by the shortest route—and, after that, oblivion, till the compelling sound of the réveille brought him out again to greet the cold dawn.

### The Men who Helped

And all the time he was blundering through to perfection there was a small army of people whose work it was to assist him in emerging from the grub stage, and to create, often from very unpromising material, the disciplined soldier, alert and self-reliant. There were officers innumerable, but the bulk of these themselves required training, being newly come to the business of soldiering.

There were the quartermasters (commissioned officers holding the honorary rank of lieutenant), who were procuring kits, clothing, and equipment; the pay officer, who was arranging his salary; the Army Service Corps, which was providing him

with his daily food; a whole legion of instructors and non-commissioned officers and commissioned officers, who had emerged from their retirement at the request of Lord Kitchener, guiding the recruit in the way he should go; doctors, who watched his feet; scientists, who prepared their toxins to guard him against that military scourge, typhoid fever. Cooks were being trained so that he might have fresh bread every day; companies of engineers were being employed that his camp might be healthy and his communications by telegraph wire and telephone be made secure. It seemed as though Britain, conscious of the nobility of effort which had brought Kitchener's Army into existence, was utilising all her care and all her strength to guard the soldier in the making from the dangers that might otherwise threaten him in his novel surroundings.

### A Bird's-eye View of a Kitchener Battalion

Taking a bird's-eye view of a battalion in the early days of the training, you might have thought there was no cohesion, and that each little party was working at something which was entirely foreign to the other. One company lying on the ground with its legs extended upward, performing trying physical evolutions, had no apparent association with the men who, in another part of the parade ground, were, with great stamping of feet, engaged in the bayonet exercise. And yet the same training came to all, and gradually the laggard recruits who had come late were reaching a stage of military perfection which would enable them to act together by companies.

And contemporaneously with this physical training, there began the spiritual creation of the young soldier. He was not taught by a book or by an instructor. He was, in this matter, the pupil of the old soldier, and the leaven of history and tradition was doing its work. The recruit began his military career with the sort of idea that one regiment was very much like another, and that there was not a pin to choose between them. If he found himself in the Wigshires, the fact only interested him because he had no idea that such a regiment had existed. If anybody had told him that the Sharpshooters would make a better regiment, he would have accepted the statement calmly, and thought possibly there must be something in it. He was neither sure of himself nor his regiment. There was soon, however, to be revealed to him in ever-increasing glory the extent of the Wigshires' wonder. Men and officers of famous regiments come and go, but its soul, its spirit, embodied in history and tradition, lives on for ever.

He learnt there were such things as battle honours, and that a certain sacred flag, which was never seen, and was, indeed, at that particular moment, reposing in the local cathedral, had inscribed upon it the names of some sixteen villages and towns in various parts of the world where the regiment and the men of the regiment of other days had secured fame and glory on the battlefield.

He learnt that his regiment was the finest marching regiment in the world; that of all the troops who had been engaged in the great war, none had behaved with such splendid valour and with such extraordinary endurance as the 1st Battalion of his particular regiment. It might not be in the papers, there might be no record of any particular accomplishment; but the thing was so, all the same.

The Kitchener soldier began to take a pride in this wonderful 1st Battalion of his, with its huge list of casualties and its fine roll of honour. And when eventually his cap badge was served out to him—there was a shortage of these in the early days—he wore it with singular pride, and would not have exchanged it for the badge of any other regiment on the earth.

Then one afternoon the adjutant of the Kitchener battalion addressed the squad, telling them that he expected them to be worthy of the 1st Battalion. He put the recruit and his fellows on their mettle. The pride of the regiment was growing slowly but strongly, and there were several hundred camps in England filled with men all exalted by a secure conviction that their Corps represented the flower and pride of the British Army.

What foundations of future regimental prestige, pride, and glory may these new regiments be laying for soldier generations yet to come!

"They are already setting standards for the coming millions," Rudyard Kipling wrote, "and have sown little sprouts of regimental tradition which may grow into age-old trees. In one corps, for example, though no dubbin is issued, a man loses his name for parading with dirty boots. He looks down scornfully on the next battalion where they are not expected to achieve the impossible. In another—an ex-Guards sergeant brought 'em up by hand—the drill is rather high-class. In a third they fuss about records for route-marching, and men who fall out have to explain themselves to their sweating companions. This is entirely right. They are all now in the Year One, and the meanest of them may be an ancestor of whom regimental posterity will say: ' There were giants in those days! ' "

THE 2ND BIRMINGHAM CITY BATTALION AT MUSKETRY PRACTICE IN SUTTON PARK.

## CHAPTER III.

### THE RECRUIT'S PROGRESS TOWARDS EFFICIENCY.

HE was a fresh-looking, sturdy youth. He stood 5 ft. 10 in. in his socks, I should say, and for all his height and breadth he was lithe and hardy.

But he was fidgety and uncomfortable.

He was in the train, and so was I, on my way home from a day spent with the new Army in the field. At every station where the train stopped he asked, in an accent which defies reproduction, "Am ah reet for Aldershot?" He had been recruited somewhere in Lancashire, and was on his way from the depôt to join his battalion, and was a stranger in a strange land. He was out of his element, almost scared, I thought, at his own boldness, as a man might be who had suddenly plunged into a new and unknown life.

The train was packed full with Kitchener men in little groups, their white canvas kit-bags reposing on the luggage-rack; Kitchener men on short leave, and Kitchener men in their rawest state journeying to their new units. Our Lancashire recruit was new enough to the game to handle his rifle gingerly and to regard with wondering interest other men like himself. "It is a fine life," he said. "Rough?" "Yes, a bit, but not so rough as you would think. The chaps you meet are grand, and the officers couldn't be better. How long do we stop at Rugby?" he asked anxiously.

He had a letter to write. I watched him finish the furtive performance as the train drew in at Rugby Station. The letter, he blushingly admitted, was to a girl. It had dropped on my knees from his fumbling, awkward fingers. As he tried to seal it a photograph of himself in his new uniform dropped out.

"She didn't mind me going away, in fact she made me enlist; and she was right. We were to be married soon—that thing's a little keepsake she wants; only had it taken yesterday." He was as excited as if he were on the way to the Front. The work at the depôt had been unusually strenuous, but he was looking forward to the work at Headquarters.

"They give you a rare gruelling at Aldershot" (he called it "The Shot," by the way, which proves he was already half a soldier), "but I can stand it, we've had marches and drill and a bit of shooting. Took me a long time to get used to this fellow," he patted his rifle, "but now I think I can manage it."

I reproduce this trivial incident, as it shows how the reality of the work and the part they were to play in the war was borne in upon these men.

In this railway carriage, with these Kitchener men, I somehow experienced a sudden sense of the urgency of the work in hand. I think it also gripped the men; one or two of them had already been in France. Some were going to finish their training there, while the others speculated as to when they would be ordered off. These were some of the men who had joined in the first rush to the recruiting offices.

I gathered from their talk something of the enormous tasks they had already accomplished. Strangers to each other, they were beguiling the time in relating stories of their experiences in the training days that now lay behind them.

There was the atmosphere of the Kitchener Army. It was working against time, everywhere haste and bustle to get ready; it was an army training for war—war already being waged in the smoking fields of France, whence came the cry for men and more men. It was a specialised training in essentials designed to fit men thoroughly, yet quickly, for the actual battlefield. Had not Kitchener said the whole of the new army was to be ready by the spring? Yes, haste was necessary, but there was to be no flurry or slipshod preparation; it was to be a fight of trained men against trained men; therefore everything must be purposeful, scientific, and thorough.

There was no suggestion of picnic in its camp life. It was an army training for the deadly business of war, and so urgently needed that there was no time for the leisurely method

AT THE SCHOOL OF MUSKETRY, HYTHE, TEACHING SNAP-SHOOTING OR RAPIDITY OF AIM, BY MEANS OF THE EYE DISC HELD TO THE INSTRUCTOR'S EY

INSTRUCTION IN RECONNAISSANCE WORK. NON-COMMISSIONED OFFICERS LEARNING TO DESCRIBE THE TOPOGRAPHY OF THE FIELD OF OPERATIONS.

be able to shoot, to dig, to march, to charge, to use his knowledge in a scientific manner, to sit a horse in certain cases, to handle his rifle, to be initiative and self-reliant, to preserve a steady nerve, and to be so inspired with *esprit de corps* that in moments of extreme danger he would think of his unit, of his regiment, before all else.

It was thus the work was going forward, orderly yet urgently and unceasingly, with the time limit and a definite end always in mind; everything was to be ready by a given date.

I saw this process going forward all over England. I saw it in Aldershot—a veritable ant-hill, where, from dawn till night, square and common, heath, hill, and valley were alive with khaki figures, all working earnestly and with a singleness of purpose wonderful to see.

Everything I saw upon the broad plains of Wiltshire, all that I witnessed upon the heather-clad lands of Hampshire, all that went on between Aldershot and Borden, between

of training of peace days. The men worked to a time-table, cramming into every available minute the tuition which experienced men were able to instil into them. Officers even came back from France to teach them some of the special wrinkles this particular war had taught.

Before taking the field every one of these new men must be an efficient soldier. He must

A LESSON IN SIGHTING.

THE 19TH BATTALION ROYAL FUSILIERS LEARNING TO AIM THEIR RIFLES AT A DUMMY TARGET.

THE PROPER WAY TO LOAD IN
THE STANDING POSITION.

Aldershot and Farnborough, was repeated in a hundred other centres. In Yorkshire, for example, on one of the wild moors, I came upon a regiment of miners. It had been recruited entirely in a great mining area, and the men spoke a dialect which was almost unintelligible to me. Splendid specimens of manhood they were, and at first I thought I had come upon a Guards' battalion. They were encamped on a gentle slope, in a valley so broad that whilst the

working in positions which, to the outsider, seemed horribly uncomfortable.

Sometimes, on a quiet stretch of the road between railway station and camp, I would come upon one of the new batteries of the Royal Field Artillery. There are 130 of these somewhere in England, and in a later number I hope to describe their training. Occasionally I would find them going into mimic action, dashing with jingle of harness and cracking of whips across rough ground to take up a position which had been chosen. Sometimes they would be proceeding solemnly between little wooden posts, turning, cantering, galloping, and walking, in order to test the driver's ability to pass between obstacles without the wheels of the guns touching them. Already these men had learned how to manage horses and guns.

And always and everywhere it was the same—an atmosphere of deadly earnestness, urgency, and concentration. The Kitchener

POLE TARGETS FORMING A SKELETON ENEMY OPERATED BY A PRIVATE.

white tents were bathed in sunlight, you could look across the valley at the rain which was falling twenty miles away. The Adjutant had been an agent of one of the great insurance houses of London. Previous to this he had been fighting in Natal, and had trained raw Kaffirs for supply work.

"There is very little difference between the men you see here and those you have seen at Aldershot," he said, "except that our men prefer trench digging to anything else!"

That was easily understandable, for these young soldiers of Kitchener's Army had served their apprenticeship in mines, and were perfectly contented when they were

enthusiast was sometimes impatient and querulous about things he reckoned did not matter. Little he knew. I was amused to hear a newcomer—a young man, lately a City stockbroker—say to an old seasoned warrior, a retired Colonel, whom he was entertaining at a village inn after a hard day's drill:

"Now tell me, Colonel, don't you think all this rifle drill is tomfoolery? We're out for business and quick training in essentials; can't they cut out all this dreary practice in 'presenting arms,' 'sloping arms,' and the rest of it? It's so much wasted time, seems to me. The trick is to be able to shoot, isn't it, and shoot straight?

A LESSON IN TRIGGER-PRESSING.

This everlasting drill is so much humbug, good enough in peace time when there is no need to hurry, but now—now hustle's the word."

"Damn it, sir," replied the ruffled Colonel, "you speak like a fool; doubtless you know something about the price of stocks and shares, but you know less than my little Scotch terrier there about what you're here for. I came down from London to see how you were getting on, and I'll take the liberty of giving you a word

SHOOTING AT A MINIATURE RIFLE RANGE.

of advice. If you'll do as you're ordered and *because* you're ordered, and trust to others to know what's right, you'll get on with your business quicker."

"Keep cool, Colonel; I'll sit at your feet and learn wisdom if you've a mind to impart it—only I expect your wisdom is of the same old red-tape order."

"You think so! You don't know I was watching you on parade this morning, young man. I watched how you handled your rifle; it was all I could do to keep from *shouting* at you. Had you ever a rifle in your hand before you came here, may I ask?"

"I don't mind saying that I never had. I'll confide a little more to you. I imagined it a pretty simple thing to raise a rifle to the shoulder and fire. I knew, of course, some practice was needed to shoot straight. I found that with the butt pressed into my

SOLDIERS CLEANING THEIR RIFLES BY POURING BOILING WATER DOWN THE BARRELS.

shoulder it was all I could do to hold the rifle with my left arm stretched out and the right crooked towards the trigger; the wretched thing had a tendency to wobble —the thing's a bit heavy, you know.

RECRUITS LEARNING TO TAKE COVER BEHIND THE BOARDS OF A POLO GROUND.

A SQUAD OF QUEEN'S WESTMINSTERS AT FIRING PRACTICE IN THE COURSE OF A SHAM FIGHT.

A MACHINE GUN SECTION TAKING COVER IN A DITCH.

Although I got the back-sight and the fore-sight in line with my object, I couldn't keep it fixed at that for a second. I had extraordinary trouble to keep the muzzle from wobbling to and fro; it would point at anything in the world except the bull's-eye, although *it* seemed to stare steadily at me from the other end of the range all the same."

"Thank heaven you have the sense to confess it. You'll soon conquer that. It was the rifle *drill*, however, we were discussing. Now let me tell you something you obviously do not know. The thing of particular value in this drill is that it *familiarises you with the rifle*—with its weight, its balance, and how to handle it so that it becomes almost part of you. No doubt you think it absurd that you, who are training hard to engage the enemy as soon as possible, should bother your head about the best way of bringing the rifle butt from the ground to the shoulder. Equally unnecessary, no doubt, to go through the complicated bayonet exercise, since your only desire is to slay your foe with the bayonet,

A CAUTIOUS ADVANCE THROUGH THICK UNDERGROWTH.

TRENCH-DIGGING IS HARD WORK, BUT THE MEN IN TRAINING GO ABOUT IT WITH LIGHT HEARTS.

LIEUT. SWAINSTON EXPLAINING TO THE QUEEN'S WESTMINSTERS THE METHODS FOLLOWED IN THE CONSTRUCTION OF A TRAVERSE DUG UNDER HIS DIRECTION AT HAMSTEAD HEATH.

and therefore it is not to be supposed that you would introduce anything of ceremony into your method of destruction. It may not have occurred to you that he may slay you.

"There's a reason for everything you're ordered to do. You've got to occupy as little space as possible, my lad. The less there is of you and your rifle, the less there is for the enemy to hit. That's why you must practise standing with your rifle close to your side. You bring your rifle to the 'slope' because that's the easiest way of carrying it."

you are able to handle it easily under all sorts of unlooked-for circumstances."

This detailed and thorough training in musketry, therefore, was one of the essentials, although some of the new Kitchener men, like the old Colonel's friend, were slow to understand the why and the wherefore of it.

The range work was now reaching its advanced stage. Targets at 600 yards were being battered day by day by companies of men, all anxious to emulate their fellows. For the keenest rivalry existed between companies, and the most extravagant

THE QUEEN'S WESTMINSTERS TRENCH-DIGGING ON HAMSTEAD HEATH.

The young man nodded in agreement.

"For equally good reason you are taught to bring your arm from the 'slope' to the 'present,' and from the 'present' to the 'order'—that is, your position at 'attention'—your rifle by your right side. And when you have mastered the peculiarities of this piece of steel and wood, and learned instinctively where the point of balance lies, and can handle it without danger to yourself or to your comrades, you are ready for exercises which necessitate the rifle being carried in the most convenient manner, and

claims were put forward nightly as to rival merits.

The recruit, who no longer regarded himself as a recruit, had got over all his earlier awkwardness with the rifle, and had learnt to resist the impulse, which every recruit has, to press the trigger at inconvenient moments. He had come to the point when he almost automatically ceased breathing when he pressed the butt into his shoulder and gently pressed—not pulled—the trigger, still keeping his sight upon the object he was aiming at, even long after the bullet had left the muzzle. A soldier pulls the trigger gently inward and upward. So doing, he exercises no jolt upon the rifle, and does not, even to a slight extent, disturb his aim.

The recruit had now mastered questions of trajectory, and the difference between the line of sight and the line of fire. "What is a trajectory?" asked the recruit, and his instructor glared, but explained with some labour: "Don't you know that the bullet does not follow the direct passage from muzzle to target, as the soldier sees it, but takes a slight curve, and reaches its billet by a downhill route?" He had learnt the necessity for holding his rifle straight, and he had been taught by painstaking instructors what happens if it is just a little askew, and he had

KITCHENER BATTALION WAITING TO FALL IN FOR A ROUTE MARCH.

become a mathematician in so far that he was able to allow for the effects of light and wind.

During the period of his recruit training —that is to say, when he was firing miniature rifles, in order to improve himself in aiming, he had fired at a variety of targets, varying from the common card target, on which his hits were plainly recorded, to the cinema target—a much more exciting experience, where he was firing at racing cyclists and getting them every time.

Naturally enough, many of the courses through which the soldier in ordinary times of preparation would have passed were necessarily condensed in order that the soldier might concentrate the whole of his attention upon matters essential.

His firing course was reduced to the smallest limit. He was initiated into the mysteries of "grouping," and learnt that it was not necessary that a man aiming at a target should hit the bull's-eye, but that it was very necessary that, wherever he hit, he should hit again. That is to say if, firing at a target, I hit it in the left-hand corner instead of the central spot which is known as the bull's-eye, I am expected, when I am "grouping," to put all the rest of my shots somewhere near my first.

Indeed, much of the old method of target firing was dispensed with, and instead, the

canvas painted to represent a distant landscape. From a distance of twenty-five yards, and taking the landscape sector by sector, he gave his opinion as to the distance each painted object represented.

"A sector, about which you hear a great deal," said his instructor, "is an area of ground which is roughly fan-shaped—t h e observer, so to speak, standing on the handle and looking toward the extended sticks of the fan."

Battle practice targets arranged in tiers, so that each tier repre-sented a further distance, were used to instruct the N.C.O. The old service bull's-eye target was a conspicuous ob-ject on a land-scape—the recruit had to judge the distances which separated him from a dingy-coloured enemy against a neutral-coloured back-

recruit was taught to shoot at a "bobbing jinny," a head and shoulders of various colours, which appeared suddenly from the earth, stayed up for a second, and was gone again.

The first sections that fired at these ap-paritions fired wildly enough, and delivered most of their bullets at a moment when the head disappeared. And this snap-shooting was one of the most valuable pieces of train-ing the recruit received.

He had to undergo a "visual training," and his military vocabulary was consider-ably enlarged.

His course of tuition began on landscape targets—that is to say on strips of card or

ground without the assistance of a range-finder.

"It is impossible to estimate distances beyond 1,200 to 1,400 yards," he was told; "below that distance you can tell the dis-tance to within a hundred yards by the size of the object. You can't go far wrong if you are any judge at all; if, when you're asked to judge, say, the distance the spire of a church is, and you say to yourself, ' The distance cannot be more than so many yards, or less than so many—I'll split the difference.' "

At night, when the area of vision was limited, he judged mainly by sound.

"You can hear the sound of marching

BRINGING IN THE WATER-WAGON.

PREPARING THE MIDDAY MEAL.

men on soft ground if you are standing. You hear them on hard ground best when you are lying down."

There were other instructions.

"Use your eyes, use your ears, use your brains. If you are scouting and you see a body of the enemy pass, count them and mark the distance they are from you. You can see a man's eyes at 100 yards, his buttons at 200 yards, his face at 300. When he's 400 yards away you can just see the movement of his legs, and the colour of his uniform at 500. If he fires at you, watch the flash of his rifle; if the report comes one second later he is 350 yards away, two seconds 700, and so on."

"But, Sergeant, how am I to count a passing enemy if he is too far off for me to see?" demanded the recruit.

"Mark a point he is passing—a tree, a house, or a telegraph-pole. Look at your watch and see how long he takes to pass a given point. If it is cavalry riding in twos, sixty will pass every minute, if cavalry at a trot, 220 to 230 pass. Guns and wagons pass five to a minute, and infantry in fours, 200."

I watched a squad at bayonet exercise, grim and terrible to anyone who thought of the deadly work that has already taken place in the great war. But obviously for the time being the men were thinking more of the fascination and fun of

THE SOLDIER IS A HANDY MAN WHO CAN TURN HIS HAND TO ANYTHING, EVEN TO A BIT OF MANGLING.

EYES FRONT! THE QUEEN'S WESTMINSTERS FACE THE FIRE OF A FAIR SHARP-SHOOTER.

it—and also, when they left off, of their tired bodies, because bayonet exercise is tiring work, without a doubt. Here was a man with the biceps of a boxer lunging for all he was worth at a dummy figure, a heavy bag packed with fibre—"Steady, my man, that is not the way to slip the bayonet into your he explained, is that which you deliver with one hand, the other hand being outstretched to balance the body.

"Then you will find that the bayonet goes in by itself. There's no necessity for putting your weight into your thrust. Simply throw up the rifle straight ahead of you, with one hand holding the small of the butt.

THERE IS PLENTY OF THE FIGHTING SPIRIT IN KITCHENER'S ARMY, AS IS SHOWN BY THE GREAT POPULARITY OF BOXING MATCHES, WHICH, SPIRITEDLY CONTESTED, ARE GREATLY ENJOYED BOTH BY COMBATANTS AND SPECTATORS.

enemy. You mustn't lurch like that. You'll overbalance yourself and then you'll find your German friend standing over you and you'll be at his mercy. Let me show you again how to do it," said the old expert.

The most effective of the bayonet thrusts, The weight of the rifle and the sharpness of the bayonet will do the rest."

So the admonished recruit started again to practise upon the heavy bags packed with fibre, and tested the accuracy of this statement. As yet, his bayonet was not sharpened, but even in a fairly blunt condition he found there was quite sufficient edge on the weapon to carry it through its objective.

But for the men, naturally enough, field operations made the most fascinating feature of their training. Into these they put all their heart and soul. The operations savoured of actual warfare, and were of absorbing interest, calling forth, as they

The British system of fighting—the outcome of experience in many little wars—is unlike any other in the world, or was, until our quick-witted enemy saw and grasped its advantage and endeavoured to imitate it. The system of fighting is that known as "open order"—a method of fighting which is foreign to the German ideals. It

did, their faculties of observation, reasoning, and intelligence. They could appreciate also the reason for things; indeed, the work fascinated the best type of men. There were so many undreamed-of things that riveted their attention; they had to use their wits.

enabled us with a very small force to hold back larger bodies of the enemy in the early days of the war.

The German officer who wrote, "The British make extraordinary use of the ground," stumbled on a truth. Our troops are able, by availing themselves of every

A PATROL OF CYCLING SCOUTS LYING IN AMBUSH UNDER COVER OF A HEDGE.

piece of cover, to hide themselves from their enemy and to shield themselves from his rifle attack.

On the Sussex Downs, on Yorkshire moors, on the heaths and hills of Surrey, in the meadows and woodlands of Essex, the men learned their lesson, haltingly at first, but later with surprising alertness. The new recruit, whose idea of "cover" was of the vaguest kind, who perhaps had visions of battlemented walls and sound concrete defences, was to learn that a hum-

veritable gifts of Providence, especially intended for the British soldier; and that even a slight unevenness of ground, a mound, a hollow, a hillock or a ditch, which he might not have noticed had he traversed it in his civilian days, gave him an immeasurable advantage over an attacker in the open, if it was properly utilised. At first, if a man did find cover—cover which was self-evident even to his amateur eyes—the chances were that he would make a wrong use of it.

"Now, men, never fire over your cover; fire round it and fire *from the right of it.*" Obvious, when you come to think of it; but not all of us think before we act, especially in the heat of battle.

"Why not from the left?" thought the recruit. His unspoken question was already answered while he was still worrying over his thought.

"If you fire from the right of cover, the whole of your body, with the exception of your rifle hand and your right shoulder and the right side of your face, is protected by the heap of stones or earth which you are using. If you fire from the left, the *whole of your body is exposed* and the cover is no use whatever. Do not forget it! Always take the right of the cover, and keep your rifle closely pressed against the bank or hayrick or door or whatever it is which is protecting you, to give your rifle greater steadiness."

Again: "When you're firing from a loophole, fire from the left; because it's not the loophole which is giving you cover, but the bit of solid steel on the left of it. If you rest your rifle against the right side of a loophole, the whole of your body is exposed to any chance shot which happens to find the gap."

From Yorkshire to Lancashire, from Lancashire to the wilds of Cumberland, from Cumberland back again to Aldershot I went, to witness the continual progress of successful effort. Aldershot and the camps about were always the more fascinating, for here one saw every branch of the service come "into action."

There on a grey winter morning I saw the men of the new Army engaged in field work.

No longer were the men addressed by spoken words of command. They had to keep alert, with eyes fixed upon the commander, watching for the signal which now took the place of the spoken word, with ears open for the shrill call of a whistle which was to change their formation. With fifty of his fellows, the recruit lay extended upon the damp earth, a little hummock serving as cover, his eyes fixed upon his commander, who was cautiously, and with body bent, moving ahead. Suddenly the arm of the officer ahead would swing from rear to front. Instantly the whole company rises as one man and moves ahead, for the signal has come to "advance."

Then the officer sees something he does not quite like. His arm shoots up and remains rigid above his head; the company halt. They detect another quick movement, as though he were patting some invisible dog. Immediately the whole sink to the ground, obedient to the signal. Then the officer's arm goes up again, and he makes two or three little circles above his head. This is the order to retire, and the company, turning about, moves back the way it came.

mock, even a blade of grass, if it screens the attacker or defender from the clear view of his adversary, was not to be despised. He learned that ditches and hedges were the

THE UNIVERSITY AND PUBLIC SCHOOL CORPS AT EPSOM HAVE TRAINED INTO A FINE BODY OF SOLDIERS.

Again the officer pats the imaginary dog, and down goes the company flat upon the ground, their faces toward the front. Again the advance signal. The clenched hand of the officer moves up and down as though he were manipulating a pump, and the company breaks into a run, since this is the signal to "double."

The company is now in extended order, the number of paces between each man being regulated by the wishes of the commander. Suddenly the officer's whistle sounds a succession of short, sharp blasts, and the extended ranks, continuing their run, close in upon their commanding officer. Mythical cavalry has been sighted, and cavalry cannot be met in extended order, but in shoulder-to-shoulder formation with the bayonet.

"Never worry about cavalry charging you," remarked a man of experience. "It doesn't very often happen in war, and it doesn't happen twice to the same cavalry."

A FULLY TRAINED COMPANY OF KITCHENER'S ARMY, FIT AND READY FOR THE FIELD.

In this ominous style did he indicate the uselessness of cavalry attacking infantry troops in close formation.

This was the beginning of the field training—a training which extended by and by to every branch of warfare and its science, as we shall see.

This "field-training" succeeded the ceremonial drill, the marching by companies, the manœuvring of sections and platoons into line, the exercises with rifle and bayonet, and the longer physical drills which were part of the daily routine in the earlier days of the recruit's service.

Field work is a general term which comprehends all the field training outside actual barrack-square training. One morning would be devoted to drill in extended order, another to the practice of the attack, yet another to the more difficult and backaching business of trench digging.

Here the recruit came upon unsuspected lines of information. He touched the fringe of real war one day when he was

engaged in extended order attack, and during an interval watched a more advanced brigade attack being delivered against a mimic enemy. The officer of his company seized the opportunity of imparting a little lecture, illustrating his points by the operations which were going on under the company's eyes.

The trenches the "enemy" were planning to attack were plainly to be seen, long, yellow scars on the dun surface of the earth. But the novice who expected to see something happen there was deceived. The fire that greeted the advancing infantry of the enemy, which poured across the ground with a yell to the attack, came from a quite unexpected quarter.

"They are attacking false trenches," explained the officer to his interested novices. "You see how cunning infantry, by turning over loose earth in regular lines, will often convey to the enemy an impression that the trenches are in a certain place. The advantage of this is that the enemy's artillery fire is drawn upon those abrasions, while his foe, remaining in well-dug and well-protected

MANY OF THE MOTOR SCOUTS OF THE AUTOMOBILE ASSOCIATION VOLUNTEERED FOR WAR SERVICE, AND ARE HERE SEEN TRAINING.

trenches, invisible to the eye, waits for the enemy to come up and then enfilades him —in other words, takes him on the flank.

"A commander has to be very careful in making his attack," the officer went on, "otherwise he will find himself throwing the whole of his strength at trenches which are only a foot or so deep, and which contain none of the enemy."

"But don't they see them digging their trenches, sir?" asked the recruit.

The officer smiled.

"They will see you digging your trench," he said, "because you will do it by day. But at the front all trench lines are dug by night, and under the cover of darkness they are not only dug, but they are screened from observation by brushwood and loose

grasses. You must always remember," he went on, "that the edge of a trench should follow, as far as possible, the natural contours of the country in which it is dug. Any straight, unnatural line will at once be seen by the enemy, and will draw his fire. Half the art of trench digging is to conceal, not only the body of the soldier from the enemy's bullets, but to hide the place in which those bodies are concealed."

These false trenches, besides, also serve the purpose of deceiving the enemy as to the numbers of the force which is opposed to him. He has to make his plans according to the information he can collect from spies, and since it is impossible for the spy to get up to the firing line without detection, there are innumerable subter-

Kitchener's battalions which had been simultaneously ordered up from Pirbright to guard the railway against the invader from Aldershot.

There was a deadly earnestness about these operations which was very impressive. Over at the back of the hills, as the column swung up the steep little road which leads to the wilderness of firs and bracken beyond, enemy guns were thundering, and to the recruit, with his twenty-five rounds of blank ammunition in his pouch, there was something of the reality and splendour of war in his furtive movements against his unseen foe.

The enemy infantry was supposed to be supported by artillery fire, and so the battalion, smartly, though without haste, was opening up into little groups fifty yards or more apart. It was the first step in an infantry attack under such circumstances, as then it was not likely that the burst of a shell would wreck harm on more than one group.

So, without confusion, keeping in touch through their platoon commanders and company officers, the attackers progressed until they were almost within range of the rifle fire of the opposing unseen infantry. They took to extended order at the shrill command of the whistle. A little later they dropped prone upon their stomachs and wormed their way along, varying this slow progression with a quick, sharp burst. This was when another signal came, and they would jump from their prone position almost as one man and tear eagerly forward, still crouching as they ran, their rifles at the trail. Another whistle—and down to earth they flopped once more, seemingly making part of the winter landscape.

They were becoming wise hands at the game of war. Not one of them took cover behind the bare and stunted shrubs that

fuges by which the agents of the enemy discover the strength of the defending troops. One way is to count the rations which are issued many miles behind the firing line—rations intended for the men in the trenches.

Very often at Aldershot there were much bigger things than company work on hand. Then réveille would bring long columns of infantry moving in the direction of Laffan's Plain, or toward the Fox Hills, looking forward eagerly to a real big field day. A mysterious enemy had established himself, holding a ridge which barred the way to London. This enemy, invested for the moment with all the malignity and desperation of the Hun, was in point of fact nothing more dangerous than a couple of

A MOTOR-CYCLIST SCOUT AND DESPATCH RIDER AT
SIGNALLING PRACTICE.

attackers' lines to report. Nearer drew the opposing lines. You saw no sign of soldiers on either side. Yet the men, crouched down level with the ground, were creeping forward persistently. But for the rattle of rifle fire, now incessant all along the line, and the unwearying crash of artillery, you might suppose that these wooded hills were innocent of soldiers. The scouts had already returned stealthily; the advance parties had fallen back, to conform with the general line; shrill whistles called in all directions; and suddenly the hills were alive with men, who rushed frantically forward; till at the shrill of whistles they again disappeared.

And so the sham fight developed to its crisis, to the successful drawing of the enemy from their position, till at last the bugle sounded "Stand fast!" and the day's fight was ended.

The pawns in the game claim their victories loudly, and dispute with some asperity the success of attack or defence, but the result was in the hands of umpires, and was communicated at a conference of officers by the general commanding—a conference where the ability or failure of individual commanders was discussed with sometimes embarrassing frankness.

In the late afternoon, as the dusk came, I again encountered this battalion of the new army. They had been out since daybreak; weary and somewhat mud-stained, they were marching along the broad highway back to camp. It may have appeared so only to imagination, because I had been greatly stirred—still, I think it was actual and real. The light of battle was still in their eyes, they had a proud and determined bearing. They had done a good day's work; they knew it, and anticipated the praise their commanding officer would bestow on them.

On this drab day in a quiet English county, it had been as near as possible the real thing. From start to finish, indeed, "war conditions" was the keynote of all the "Kitchener's Army" training. It was a training, first, last, and all the time, in the essentials of war. It could hardly be otherwise. Had not Lord Kitchener said that the new armies were to take the field by the Spring?

Once more that day I was to see them. This time it was at an evening lecture.

here and there dotted the level plain. For this reason, that it was safer to fall straight to earth. Every definite object, such as one of these trees, made an easy target, and its exact range would be certain to have been marked by the men in the trenches they were attacking. The men of the attacking army knew the little things that matter in the great game of war.

Now the scouts had come into action. You could hear the rattle and crash of musketry, and then the staccato note of the new machine-gun section.

High in the air circled a buzzing aeroplane, noting, locating, and from time to time swooping back on the

The driving rain was lashing the window-panes of the hall, which had been a skating rink. There were men there, I know, with blistered hands and aching back—the legacy from digging trenches. Others who had been in the sham fight still smelt of the grassy earth on which they had crouched and crawled. The fascination of the game he was learning had gripped the Kitchener man, and, in spite of his fatigue and aching limbs, he listened with the keenest appreciation to those lessons in the thousand subterfuges of war. They might only be little points, but he greedily took them all in, storing them up for future use when the day came.

It is safe to say that no Kitchener soldier will ever forget in his after life the thrill and the joy of those early-morning fights, under grey skies, with the bite of snow in the air and the dark background of gaunt trees to introduce the atmosphere and gloom of war.

He will not forget the bivouacs, when the Kitchener battalions moved out at night and marched in silence across country to take up their position at dawn; the whispered conversations; the doze into which he fell when he was given little half-hour spells of rest. Stumbling through the night, led sometimes by a disc fastened to a pole—a disc covered with luminous paint, which was visible only to those who marched in the rear—and sometimes by the more primitive process of keeping in touch with the foremost file, he marched on, hour

'BILLY' THE GOAT MASCOT OF THE WELSH REGIMENT, MARCHED PROUDLY WITH THE TROOPS WHEN THEY WERE REVIEWED BY THE KING.

LEARNING HOW TO THRUST WITH THE BAYONET.

after hour, till the dawn came, and, with the dawn, his surprise attack.

Some of the camps were kept under war conditions, and occasionally a commanding officer would receive, perhaps in the middle of the night, the startling information that an enemy force was moving on his position. From tent to tent hurried the orderly sergeant, urgently calling the men to parade, and the defenders' line would be hardly formed before the advance scouts of the attacker were in touch.

Sometimes no such warning came to him, and the first intimation that a neighbouring camp, or one some twenty miles away, was harbouring unfriendly designs, came in the shape of the wild shots which the outposts were firing. In this connection a very amusing story came to me. Between two camps in the north of England there existed a rivalry which could only be described as deadly. Surprise attacks upon one side or the other were of constant occurrence, and

all this went on with the full approval, indeed with the commendation, of the general officer commanding, who watched the growth of this proper war spirit with every satisfaction. It came so that the men in one camp did not undress when they retired to their tents, until they were absolutely certain that the men of the other camp were so engaged in some general scheme of tactics that no attack was to be feared.

Both sides employed spies, and both went to extraordinary lengths in order to bamboozle the other. Once the northern camp, moving down by night to surprise their enemy, were met half way by a devastating fire, the enemy having received information in time to establish trench lines half way between the two camps. On another occasion the southern camp attempted a secret attack, and by dint of hard marching came up to the "enemy" an hour before dawn, only to find that his tents had entirely vanished, the whole camp having been shifted overnight, with the exception of a few store tents. Returning somewhat dispirited and probably a little amused by the "enemy's" cunning, the troops marched back to their own camp, only to be met by a withering fire from the northern army, which had made a wide detour in the night and seized the camp of the attacker, and was now holding it against him.

Such exercises as these, duplicating as they did many of the actual conditions which the soldier would be asked to face, made splendid training for the young soldier. They heartened even the newest of the recruits, and brought him into line with his older comrades. The value of this was immeasurable, for the levelling up of the newer recruits to the standard of those who had had four or five months of training, was one of the difficulties of commanding officers, who were constantly finding raw civilians on their hands who, from necessity, must often be included in tactical schemes which required all the experience of the "old soldier."

But there is no tutor like the trained man, and a duffer who found himself between two "knowing" privates learnt more in a couple of days of actual "warfare" than he could have learnt in the same number of weeks upon the barrack square.

Tricks of trench work especially appealed to the Kitchener soldier, since the great war had developed so largely into a vast conflict of entrenchments. One little bit of knowledge he acquired will serve as an example. All that one can see of a barbed wire entanglement before a trench in most instances are the upright posts to which the wire, invisible from any distance, is fastened. Therefore, in preparing dummy trenches there was no need for him to make elaborate pretence or to put strings in place of wire. All that was necessary to do was to place wooden posts at intervals, and these were quite sufficient to deceive an attacking force into believing that wire exists. The Kitchener man was taught how to build

A MACHINE-GUN SECTION UNDER COVER, WAITING TO GIVE THE ENEMY'S PATROL A SURPRISE.

ENGINEERS BEING GIVEN INSTRUCTION AT HENLEY IN THE METHOD OF
CONSTRUCTING A PONTOON BRIDGE.

the most effective form of parapet, and "parados" against rear fire,
how to make traverses, how to construct "head cover" with any
material he could scratch together.

"Where shall I get material?" The recruit had not yet got out
of the habit of asking questions.

"Anywhere—cut that bush—take an axe and fell that tree—hi,
you! take your bill-hook and cut the grass. Not in front of the
trench, you idiot! Do you want the enemy to spot the cleared
space? Besides, grass is cover." For this purpose every regiment
has in its equipment bill-hooks, reaping-hooks, and axes.

The lessons of the great war would be the subject most often
chosen in the lectures he listened to, and some particular attack
or defence, details of which had been received, would be used to
illustrate the advantage of some variety of tactics. A blackboard
and a piece of chalk would illustrate the futility of certain kinds
of defences, and would show the recruit how the popular idea of
a trench was not only valueless, but dangerous to the man who
used it to shield himself against the bullets of the enemy.

Well, indeed, did the soldier of the new army learn the lesson
which his wise masters taught him, and learned it all the more
readily since there was going on under his very eyes the practice
and proof of all this teaching.

If anything, the training Kitchener's Army received was even
more valuable than the training which the regular soldier had
experienced during peace time. The object lessons the war
afforded constantly, in the craft of the soldier, gave an additional

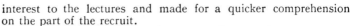

interest to the lectures and made for a quicker comprehension on the part of the recruit.

No section of battalion workers were of greater importance, not only so far as the effective fighting strength of the regiment was concerned, but from the point of view of physique and efficiency, than the machine-gun section. We started the war with a considerable shortage of machine-guns, and learned to our cost that every German battalion could produce two, and sometimes four, to our one. We had learned the value of concentrated Maxim-gun fire, and, since this weapon is a complicated instrument, requiring careful and technical handling, the men of the new machine-gun sections were chosen for their physique, alertness, and intelligence.

In most of the newer battalions the section manœuvred with a wooden gun, the necessary Maxims not being available for some considerable period. Drawn by mules, which earned for the man told off for the care of this animal the ironic title of "trooper," the gun team had to learn many other things than the actual mechanism of the gun. The Maxim is practically a rifle with an automatic breach action. To prevent the rifle barrel becoming over-heated, it is enclosed in a brass water-jacket, and ammunition is fed to the breach by means of canvas belts carrying supplies of cartridges.

The recoil of one shot loads and fires the next cartridge, and so on *ad infinitum*, or until the belt is exhausted. This is a very rough description of the very complicated mechanism of the machine-gun, but describes, in general terms, the principle of the weapon.

PRACTISING THE BUILDING OF RAFTS AND BRIDGES. THE PICTURE SHOWS THE SKELETON OF A CASK BRIDGE BEING LAUNCHED.

THE MIDDLESEX IMPERIAL YEOMANRY HAVE BEEN ENGAGED ON WIMBLEDON COMMON IN THE WORK OF BREAKING IN REMOUNTS FOR THE ARMY.

The actual handling of the gun was mastered soon enough by these eager young men who had volunteered for the work—more dangerous than the ordinary infantry work, because the rattle of a Maxim usually makes its presence known, and usually offers the enemy very few difficulties in the way of locating its exact position. In addition to this, the steam from the water-jacket is also liable to betray its presence, and call upon the devoted "gunners" the fire of enemy artillery.

The No. 1 of the gun—he who actually fires and sights the weapon—must be an excellent shot, for if he misses, he misses not only with one round, but with ten or twenty. The recruit learned the value of Maxim fire, one of the most potent factors in surprise attacks, and a most powerful infantry arm for covering retirements or assisting advances of infantry.

"If your gun jams—which means if a cartridge misses fire or refuses to come out after firing—you are a dead man," said the instructor. "See that every cartridge is in its place in the belt. A little carelessness will cost you your life—and, what is more important, may mean the loss of the gun to the enemy."

Grasping the two brass handles of the gun and pressing the double button which controls the fire, the gunner can sweep whole areas clean, and, thanks to its mobility, it is possible to carry it on its tripod or wheel it on its light carriage across country which would be impracticable for heavy artillery.

It is not generally known by civilians that in some of the sham attacks such as I have described, a wooden rattle, in the style of the old police rattle, which faithfully produces the sound of Maxim fire, was often employed to indicate the presence of that weapon and to accustom Company officers to give their commands in a tone which would rise above the din of firing.

"There were three kinds of machine-gun fire," the recruit was told, "ranging fire, in which from ten to twenty rounds are 'loosed off' with the object of securing the range; rapid fire, when the greatest volume of fire is required. This does not necessarily mean an absolutely continuous fire. It is necessary after every fifty rounds to pause a little while in order to make certain that the sights are right. And, lastly, traversing fire, which is employed with the object of 'spraying' as wide a front as possible."

The machine-gunner largely depends for his instructions upon semaphore signals. Observers would signal "P," to mean that

the bullets are striking fifty yards beyond the target; and "M" (meaning *minus,* as the other means *plus*) that it is fifty yards short of the target. With Kitchener's Army came into existence a new variety of machine-gun, the weapon being carried as a side-car to a motor-cycle. The advantage of this new arm had not been fully tested, but it was obviously an extremely important addition to the equipment of a regiment.

The word "gun" is sometimes loosely employed to describe the machine-gun.

"Gun," however, invariably means cannon, and the training of the new artillery was one of the most important of Lord Kitchener's tasks.

Artillery has played a great part in the war, and we shall see in the next chapter how men were trained to follow in the footsteps of heroic "L" Battery and the splendid batteries of the Royal Field Artillery, which upon a dozen fields have maintained the high traditions of "The Royal Regiment."

To watch the amazing work which was going on all over the country was to experience some of the sensations which a dumbfounded French Minister of War confessed on the occasion of his visit to England. M. Millerand said that he was simply astounded at the wonderful results that had been obtained with Britain's new army.

Dealing with the visit of the French Minister of War to England, a leading Parisian newspaper said:—"It is not the number of men already with the colours or flowing into the recruiting offices which most impressed M. Millerand, but their physical and moral qualities and the remarkable degree of per-

UNDER SUSPICION. A PHOTOGRAPH IS CHALLENGED BY A SENTRY, AND HAS TO UNDERGO A SEARCHING
CROSS-EXAMINATION BY A SERGEANT.

CROSSING THE CROSS-TREES IS A BALANCING FEAT OF NO SMALL DIFFICULTY, BUT IT IS ONE OF THE THINGS A RECRUIT
HAS TO LEARN.

fection of their training. He was able to ascertain that, from a physical point of view, the troops he saw at Aldershot, and also at Epsom, could not be surpassed. Not only are these men of a high physical standard, however. The five months which they have spent in camp, training day and night, and in every kind of weather, under conditions which—except for shells and bullets—were practically the same as those experienced by their comrades at the front, have turned them into trained soldiers. There can be no doubt that these British armies are equal to the best."

MOTOR-BUSES READY TO TAKE THE RECRUITS' EQUIPMENT TO CAMP.

A GROUP OF SMILING RECRUITS.

## CHAPTER IV

### THE ARTILLERYMAN IN THE MAKING—HORSEMANSHIP AND GUNNERY— WITH THE ENGINEERS.

SIMULTANEOUSLY with the progress of the training of the new Kitchener infantry regiments for the great struggle which lay ahead, other recruits, drafted into different arms of the service, were as quickly and as steadily drilling and being made ready to assist the infantry when the time came. A story is told by General Sir Robert Baden-Powell that on one occasion, when he was visiting the Kaiser and witnessing, with his Imperial host, the great German manœuvres, the Emperor Wilhelm said to him : "I cannot understand how the English group their arms. You always put your artillery to the right of the line, as being first in importance; next to that you put your cavalry and your engineers; and, holding the least important place, the infantry. Now, in my army, we always put the infantry first, and we regard all other arms as so many servants to the infantry."

Sir Robert's witty reply was that the arms were placed in that order of importance— artillery, cavalry, engineers, infantry, etc.— because we grouped them alphabetically.

This war has perhaps decided the truth of the Kaiser's statement that the infantry was the principal arm, and masses of foot soldiers the principal factors in the decision of battles, and that all other services were, indeed, auxiliary. Excellent advantage as

the possession of a preponderance of guns gives to an army, it is, after all, a mechanical advantage, easily reinforced and fairly easily replaced when lost. This is not the case with the *personnel* of the service, with the young and physically sound men, the supply of which is not inexhaustible.

Yet the tremendous importance of the guns in modern warfare can scarcely be exaggerated, and Lord Kitchener and his lieutenants industriously began at a very early stage to create great artillery forces and prepare them for war.

When we talk of "guns" we, of course, refer to cannon. People sometimes speak of rifles as guns, just as they speak of machine-guns, that is to say, Maxims, as guns. But the gun when referred to in the course of this article is the 18½ pounder quick-firing cannon which is used by the Royal Field Artillery. There is another branch of the artillery—the Royal Horse Artillery (armed with a 13-pounder), and some confusion may arise in the mind of the reader, unversed in the ways of the Army, as to the difference between the "field" and the "horse." Both are, strictly speaking, horse artillery batteries. The Royal Horse Artillery, which is our crack artillery, employ a gun which is much lighter than that which is to be found in

THE HONOURABLE ARTILLERY COMPANY AT GUN PRACTICE IN THE SHELTER OF A THICKET IN RICHMOND PARK.

the field. The gunners are, moreover, mounted on horses, as distinct from the gunners of the Royal Field Artillery, who have šeats on the limber and carriage of the gun. The Royal Horse Artillery is intended for mobility and speed, and horse artillery batteries usually accompany cavalry when they are engaged in distinct operations.

Under the heading of Field Artillery are included the larger guns, the howitzers and siege guns of all kinds, used in the field.

A third branch of the artillery is the Garrison Artillery. These men are, as a rule, employed only on defensive fortress positions. For instance, all the great armaments of Gibraltar are worked by garrison artillerymen; and in that fortress there are no field or horse artillery of any kind. Men of the garrison artillery are, however, occa-

BRINGING UP THE GUNS. – A SMART BATTERY OF FIELD ARTILLERY ON THE MARCH.

moment exclude the Garrison Artillery, which was certainly strengthened by a number of new men and by Territorial troops, even though the new men were enlisted on the same terms as the remainder of Kitchener's Army—namely, for the duration of the war or for three years—and although they can, in truth, be included under the same head.

We may also pass over the heavier batteries and the more scientific branch of artillery, and

sionally employed with the heavy gun batteries in the field.

Therefore, when we are considering the new forces which Lord Kitchener created, we may for the

'ACTION FRONT!'

come to the Royal Field Artillery for our examination of the training and substance of the new arm. The Army List gives us particulars of some 130 batteries of Field Artillery, and to these must be added the large number of reserve batteries of Royal Horse Artillery.

The Kitchener recruit's introduction to this branch of the Army depended either upon his expressed inclination for service with the gunners or upon his physical qualifications. Since the horses which draw the guns have quite enough work to do to get these weapons from place to place, it is obviously desirable that the men who ride three of the six horses constituting a gun team should be as light as possible. Therefore, for the drivers of the new artillery, short and light

THE PREPARATORY STAGES OF THE WORK OF THE GUNS – BATTERIES OF ARTILLERY FORMING UP TO COME INTO ACTION.

men were chosen. For the gunners, a height standard, superior to what is required for the infantry, is laid down, a higher standard of physique being necessary in men who have to lift weights, and must be necessarily called upon to perform heavier manual labour than their brethren of the infantry.

A gun is drawn by six horses, the nearside horses being ridden, and the gun itself consists of the limber, the caissons, containing the shells, etc., and the gun itself. That is only the roughest description, but it will probably serve the non-technical reader.

In conversation with members of the fine body of men who joined the Artillery, I was impressed by the way they had followed the events of the war, and especially the gallant work of the Royal Artillery. Certainly there was much to be learnt from the war which was being waged concurrently with their training, there were splendid examples to be faithfully followed. The Royal Horse and the Royal Field Artillery had figured in every one of the earlier engagements, and "every battery had done the work of six," to use the words of a General in commending the conduct of the regiment. The retreat from Mons had been accomplished by the British Army only with the aid and by the superhuman effort of the Artillery. Gallant "L" Battery of the Royal Horse Artillery had served the guns to its last man, and by its devotion had succeeded in holding in check the major portion of Von Kluck's advance regiment. In the dust of summer, amidst the gales and rains of winter, the tireless batteries were constantly on the move, the cracking whip of the driver sounded across the sodden fields of Flanders as the stained and discoloured

limbers swayed and bumped over ploughed field and ditch. There was hardly a little copse or wood in the North of France that the Royal Artillery had not utilised to hide their guns, to veil the presence of their precious weapons from enemy airmen who moved above them backwards and forwards with an inquiring eye. Never an infantry charge developed but Artillery support had first made the assault possible.

In one particular instance we were told in a despatch from the Front:—"For ten minutes the Royal Artillery shelled a patch of ground, their shells falling with extraordinary accuracy, and bursting with a precision which was almost marvellous. They made possible the assault which the Guards Brigade delivered at the expiration of that time."

The same thing might with equal truth be said of every attack which the British Infantry delivered. Courage, precision, high technical skill, contempt for fatigue, and a heroism in danger and in time of trial beyond all understanding, these were the characteristics of the Royal Artillery, and these were the traditions which the new recruit assimilated as part of his training.

Their enthusiasm in the technical detail of the guns, in the care of their horse teams, the saddling, harness, and the rest of it, was a thing to marvel at. It was natural that men and horses, both new to each other, and both equally new to work required of a Royal Artillery Regiment, should not always see eye to eye. I think it was Rudyard Kipling who said in those days that, travelling over the countryside, he occasionally saw "men and horses arguing with each other for miles." No wonder. I know not what civilian work these horses had been engaged on, or where they were

FIELD ARTILLERY AT GUN DRILL NEAR WINDSOR.

browsing on quiet summer pastures when the call of King and Country reached them, and they found themselves suddenly commandeered for war. But I know that these men—when I saw them, expert horsemen and finished artillery men—were, only a short six months back, packers and warehousemen, clerks and salesmen, engineers and mechanics, and such like, in London, Manchester, and other large towns, and small towns, too, for that matter. The war had only been six months old when a warehouseman of W. H. Smith & Sons, the great newspaper distributors, gained a D.C.M. for conspicuous gallantry in Belgium, and a typist in the employ of George Newnes, Ltd., the publishers of the *Strand Magazine* and this periodical I am now

A GUN UNDER COVER. AN ARTILLERYMAN IS RECEIVING ORDERS BY TELEPHONE.

writing, was mentioned in the despatches of Admiral Beatty, and was also awarded the D.C.M. for gallant work on board the *Tiger*. So, doubtless, many other gallant gunners will be honoured when their day comes, for no work calls for greater bravery and single-handed pluck than that of the men behind the guns.

The earlier drill of the Artillery recruit, so far as physical exercises and squad drill were concerned, did not differ in any material degree from that which was the experience of the infantryman.

For route marches there was no necessity, as he would not be called upon to walk, though most of the recruits were exercised

sergeant of his section. The recruit was to discover that, in addition to being the friend of man, the horse could also be a source of interminable trouble. Our recruit had assumed the cares and responsibilities which usually only come to the parents of young families; for his horse's temper, his cleanliness, his hunger or his thirst, were matters to which he was called upon to give his constant attention. The feet of the beast —and Providence had very unkindly endowed him with four—needed examination and picking; he had to be brushed with the right hand and steadied with the left; and for his toilet certain inflexible rules were laid down to which the recruit must adhere,

## THE ACTION OF SHRAPNEL EXPLAINED IN DIAGRAM.

TIME FUSE SHRAPNEL.—The shell, fired from gun at right against entrenched infantry, bursts about 80 yards in front of the latter and about 15 feet above the ground. The short lines indicate the zone covered by the bullets.

PERCUSSION SHRAPNEL.—The shell, fired from gun at right against advancing infantry, bursts upon hitting the ground, throwing a shower of bullets at approaching men. It is also used against buildings, but is ineffective on soft ground.

CASE (SHRAPNEL) SHOT.—Used at short range against cavalry. The shell bursts immediately after leaving the gun. At 200 yards range the lateral spread is 25 yards.

in good, smart tramps to shape their muscles.

Nor was there bayonet exercise, nor a great deal of time spent upon the rifle range. The business of the artillery driver was to get his gun to the appointed place in the shortest possible time, and the job of the gunner was so to lay and direct his fire that he could produce the greatest execution with the smallest expenditure of ammunition. To these ends the training of the artillery recruit was directed.

Let us first take the case of the driver, with whom no time was lost in introducing him to his "two long-faced friends," as his horses were humorously described by the

or earn a sharp reprimand from his watchful sergeant. The orders were strict.

"You must start brushing your horse at the off-hand right quarter, and progress steadily toward the head, moving your brush in a circular motion with the coat and against it. You must then cross to the near side of the horse (which is his left side) and brush him on top and underneath, brush his legs, and finally add the last finishing touches on mane and tail. If he comes in wet from a parade" —and he mostly did in the early days of the Kitchener Army training—"he must be cleaned before this brushing commences."

Half an hour before the infantry réveille sounded, the trumpets of the artillery were calling the men to the stables or to the horse lines, which had to be cleaned and made tidy. The first attention to the friend of man took the shape of a rub down with a handful of straw and a quick brush over tail and mane. After that the horse must have his breakfast before the young Kitchener soldier could attend to the requirements of his own inner man. After parade and the removal of the harness, he must make a very careful inspection for galls and scratches, and report to his sergeant. More food, more water followed, before the recruit was dismissed to his own well-earned dinner.

The same ceremony was gone through at night, when the horse was made snug till the following morning. Horses, like human beings, are unequal in temper, but woe betide the unfortunate recruit who so far forgets himself as to retaliate upon his too restless or obstinate charge. Kindness to your horse is the first order of the day

in the artillery, and if there is any other strict injunction, it is that the animals shall not be fed without specific orders.

Running concurrently with his tuition in the care of horses was another kind of training, which was even more startling. He had perhaps come into the Army with no other knowledge of a horse than that it had a number of legs and was of a certain shape, and figured in all the public statues erected to great military commanders. He had not ridden a horse, though it seemed easy enough, and perhaps he looked forward to his first experience at the riding school with keen pleasure.

He was a fortunate man if he looked forward to his second experience in the same hopeful spirit. He was taught how to mount. He was given a bare-back horse, inured to the awkwardness of young recruits, and a riding master, with a clarion voice and an eagle eye which detected every lapse of the apprehensive horseman, directed him to adopt certain attitudes which, from the point of view of the recruit,

THE FIELD (HOWITZER BATTERY) ARTILLERY BRINGING THEIR HEAVY GUNS UP A STIFF SLOPE, HARD WORK FOR MEN AND HORSES BOTH.

were as unnatural as they were uncomfortable.

"Keep your toes in, your elbows to the side, and your hands down; head up, chest out, and look to your front," roared the riding master.

A very simple position to take, you might think, but one which was foreign to all the natural desires of the young rider. Much more easy it was for him to put his heels against the horse's sides, his elbows in the air, and his chin forward on his breast, ready at a moment's notice to grab the mane of his charger. He was all wings and heels in those early days; a sore trial to himself and an object of scorn to all well-trained horsemen. In certain of the cavalry regiments he gained his first experience from riding a mechanical horse, which did no more than sway about in a very encouraging manner. Of the training in other regiments, there were dark rumours of a mechanical horse which kicked and bucked and jumped in the most natural and embarrassing style. Artificial horses can do no

more than teach a man the proper position in which to hold his legs and his elbows. They can teach him to sit with a straight back and his head up: they can teach him, too, the method of grasping the reins so as to leave one hand free to manipulate the short whip—for all the world like a dog-whip—with which he will control the second of the horses under his charge.

But none of these artificial methods duplicated or reproduced in a life-like manner the curious gyrations which an able-bodied horse, with a full flow of animal spirits and a keen sense of equine humour, can develop at a moment's notice. To hold the mane of a horse is a natural and instinctive action, which the Kitchener recruit inherited from his barbarous ancestors, but the riding master, representing civilisation, ruled it otherwise.

"You fellows want a bicycle handle," he said bitterly. "I suppose you want us to breed a new kind of horse for you, Driver Jones. Let go that mane! How would you like somebody to be holding on to your

hair? Sit up and balance yourself. You can't fall off."

Driver Jones instantly confounded h i s instructor b y taking a wild toss on to the tan floor of the riding school.

It is not too much to say that the recruit without a knowledge of horses expects a fall from a horse to be followed by instant death; but the accidents in r i d i n g schools are few and far b e t w e e n, and mostly occur to the experienced "rough-riders," who are qualified to handle the least ruly of horses, and occasionally meet an animal who is particularly difficult to master.

Nevertheless, t h e terrors of the riding school were very real to the most enthusiastic recruit. This god-like instructor who sat his horse as though he was part of it was very difficult to please. "I shall never make a horseman of you, Driver Smith," h e said bitterly, "until somebody invents a horse you can ride inside!"

WHAT KITCHENER'S ARMY HAS DONE IN TRAINING – ENTRENCHMENTS ON THE EAST COAST MADE BY OUR RECRUITS.

"I thought I was getting it all right, sir," said the doleful recruit.

"All right!" scoffed his superior. "Why, if there was a looking-glass here, and that horse could see who was riding him, he would die of shame!"

It was when the Kitchener recruit came into the open with his charge, that some of his painfully acquired confidence began to desert him. He regarded a horse as a beast which had an uncontrollable passion for running away. In the riding school his eccentricities in this direction were restricted by four walls. With the whole world to range in, anything might happen to a horse with a passion for travel, and on the open spaces, where the recruit learnt to jump his horse over small obstacles, and to accom-

pany the animal in this exercise, the danger seemed increased fourfold. The criticisms of his superior were good-natured enough.

There was an undercurrent of sarcasm which set the whole of the unhappy school grinning, yet with the consciousness that they themselves might next be the object of the riding master's vitriolic comment. Yet men who had never touched a horse found pleasure and exhilaration in their new experience. "I didn't know there was so much fun in life," said an ex-typist. One recruit ventured to ask a rough-riding corporal who was instructing him how to "jump" what value this training had.

"We shan't have to jump hedges with guns, shall we, Corporal?"

He learnt, to his surprise, that something of the sort was indeed expected of him. "Go the shortest way" is the Royal Artillery motto. A hedge, a ditch, or a seemingly inaccessible hill, rocks, boulders, even small streams are obstacles which the Royal Field Artillery all but despise. "Your job," said the instructor, "is to get there. If it is necessary, you must take your gun up the side of a house and unlimber on the roof."

As day passed day, the confidence of the young rider grew. He found, as all new riders do, that it is much easier to ride a bare-backed horse than to sit a saddle; and presently he began to feel at home even when riding one horse and directing another by his side. Presently he had left the riding school or *ménage* (a riding school in the open), and was manœuvring dummy limbers across the parade ground, to his own and his officers' satisfaction.

The work of the horse-soldier in Kitchener's Army was more difficult than in ordinary times. For this reason—that he had to deal with untrained horses. All the trained horses in the kingdom had been dispatched to the Front, where they were most needed. The horses for the new Army's training were all "unmade."

Many of them were wholly wild and unmanageable. This applied to horses from Canada, but more especially to the remounts which the Argentine sent to the Army. It was wholly beyond the average Kitchener recruit's ability to master these seemingly untamable beasts, and the work

CONSTRUCTING AN EMPLACEMENT FOR A HEAVY GUN.

THE ENGINEERS NOW IN TRAINING IN ENGLAND HAVE GLORIOUS TRADITIONS TO LIVE UP TO. AT THE FRONT
THE WORK OF THE ENGINEERS HAS BEEN ONE OF THE WONDERS OF THE WAR, AND THE PICTURE ABOVE
VIVIDLY PORTRAYS MERELY ONE OF THE MANY DANGEROUS ENTERPRISES THEY ARE CALLED UPON TO
PERFORM. BARBED-WIRE ENTANGLEMENTS BETWEEN THE ALLIES AND GERMAN TRENCHES CAN ONLY BE
CONSTRUCTED AT NIGHT-TIME, AND EVEN THEN THE FRIENDLY DARKNESS IS OFTEN DISPELLED BY THE ENEMY'S
MAGNESIUM FLARES, IN THE LIGHT OF WHICH THE ENGINEERS ARE AN ALL-TOO-EASY MARK FOR THE GERMAN
SHARP-SHOOTERS.

THE CAVALRY RECRUITS TAKE THEIR FIRST LESSONS IN HORSEMANSHIP ON WOODEN STEEDS.

of taking the horses in hand and breaking them in fell to the lot of specially picked Kitchener men under the instruction of "rough-riding" corporals. The horse's

BEFORE THE EDUCATION OF A CAVALRYMAN IS COMPLETE HE MUST BE ABLE TO SIT HIS HORSE IN EVERY CONCEIVABLE WAY.

ability to buck-jump—that is to say, to spring upright in the air with his forefeet rigidly extended—is not so much an acquirement peculiar to North American mustangs as an instinct which even the best-conducted horses possess. The amateur rough-riders experienced unpleasant half-hours before they coaxed their new charges to a sense of decorum. Three or four days' work with a breaking-in saddle, which is a saddle specially prepared and weighted, brought

LEARNING THE CORRECT SEAT ON A DUMMY HORSE.

A SPLENDID JUMP BY A BRITISH CAVALRY OFFICER.

the horse to a sense of his responsibilities, and though he still evinced an occasional desire to rid himself of his human burden, he very soon adapted himself to the new conditions of life to which fate had brought him.

One of the dangers which the Kitchener cavalryman had to guard against was the liability of his horses to stampede. With this possibility in his mind, he paid more than usual attention to the picketing of his horse at night. Horses in the field are picketed to long ropes, which are staked close to the ground, and to these the halter-ropes are attached. In some cases, where it is necessary to keep a horse apart, this system of tying him up for the night is varied by hobbling him. A strap is placed round the foot of the horse, and attached to this is a rope fastened to a picket peg. (You may also "hobble" a horse by connecting one fore and one hind foot with a length of rope, which does not allow him to gallop freely.) In spite of the careful scrutiny of fastening and knot, a stampede will sometimes occur. An excitable horse, in his terror, will wrench himself free and begin a wild scamper through the darkness, taking everything that comes in his way—tent and fence—and, just as hysteria will run through a girls' school, so will panic communicate itself to the whole of the horse lines, and before the horse sentries can get their charges under control, a wild mass of panic-

NON-COMMISSIONED OFFICERS AT NETHERAVON PRACTISING A CHARGE – DUMMY SOLDIERS REPRESENTING THE ENEMY.

stricken beasts goes galloping through the darkness, and the whole camp is called up to attack the long and difficult task of recapturing the fugitives. Stampedes on any large scale are not of frequent occurrence, and it is well that they should not be, because the loss in horse-flesh is very considerable, apart from the injury which

JUST WHAT HE WANTED. THE HORSE'S DINNER-TIME AT THE FAMOUS POLO STABLES AT RANELAGH, NOW BEING USED BY THE MIDDLESEX YEOMANRY.

the animals inflict upon the hapless inmates of tents which stand in the path of their flight. After a big stampede, and when the horses are rounded up, there are generally a dozen or more who are so badly injured that they have to be destroyed. A stampede is always followed by a court of enquiry to find the cause. It is an event of regimental significance, to be remembered and guarded against in the future.

In exceptional circumstances the recruit found himself in clover. This was when he was billeted, and when his horse enjoyed the same privilege, sharing in some cases the honour of companionship with thoroughbreds in a fashionable racing stable, and in some cases taking his place in a vacant stall by the side of a domestic cow in a villager's dilapidated stable.

The gunner's progress was as rapid as that of his cavalry comrade.

The Kitchener gunner was as keen

to become proficient in his work as was the infantryman of the new Army. The driver must, in addition to his gunnery, master the business of horse manage-

POLISHING UP FOR PARADE.

ment; but in the field artillery the gunner devoted the whole of his time to learning the mysteries of his gun. Whilst the driver was having little horse tips drilled into his head, and was being taught that slack traces constituted disgraceful evidence of his bad riding, that spurs were for the horse he rode and the whip for the off horse, and that wheel drivers—that is to say, the driver who is nearest the limber— must neither be behind-hand nor beforehand, the gunner was thread-ing his way through a different and, as it seemed to him, a more complicated maze.

He learnt that his sergeant was called No. 1, and that most of

LIKE THE CAVALRYMAN, THE CAVALRY HORSE IS PERFECTLY TRAINED. HE WILL LIE DOWN AT COMMAND, AND IS THEREFORE ABLE TO TAKE AS MUCH ADVANTAGE OF COVER AS HIS MASTER.

A FIELD DAY AT RICHMOND PARK. – OFFICERS OF THE MIDDLESEX HUSSARS CLEARING A DITCH.

the important duties in action were delegated to this official. He, "No. 1," was responsible for the entire service of the gun, laying for direction, and signalling to the section officer when the gun was ready for firing. No. 2, the next important person, would attend to the breech of the gun and to the brake, and would report when the gun was loaded and the breech was closed. He, with No. 3, would help to unlimber and limber up—that is to say, to unhook the gun from the caisson when the gun was coming into action, and would help replace it when action was closed. No. 3 also attended to the telescope and dial sights.

HOW THE RECRUIT LEARNT SWORDSMANSHIP – FENCING LESSONS AT THE CAVALRY SCHOOL.

No. 4 loaded. No. 5 issued ammunition and set the fuses. No. 6 assisted. Nos. 7, 8, and 9 remained with the wagons, to assist the supply of ammunition and replace casualties, whilst No. 10 acted as coverer, and rode alongside the first-line wagon.

In the case of Horse Artillery, two men are detailed to hold the gunners' horses, but this was not necessary in the R.F.A.

Working day by day, and night by night, there came a time when a battery became a coherent shape, with every man acquainted with his duties, and a piece in the jigsaw puzzle which made the perfect whole.

The effect of fire was carefully explained. Lectures formed a very material part of the Kitchener artillery-man's training. He was taught the proportion of shrapnel that goes to explosive shell—the British had 25 per cent. high explosive and 75 per cent. shrap-nel at the beginning of the war—and the functions of the artillery were very carefully explained to him. He was shown how that wizard of artillery, the shrapnel shell, could be so arranged by means of a time-fuse that it would burst to the fraction of a second of calculation; and the science of judging dis-tances was taught, both in theory and in practice.

As important was his tuition in the use of cover.

Cover is indispensable to the artillery, cover for limbers, cover for the horses, and cover for the guns, and the recruit learnt how field pieces might be con-cealed by the judicious employment of bracken and grass, and how even the smallest copse could effec-tively disguise and conceal from the enemy and his airmen the presence of horses. Be the guns ever so well concealed, it was quite possible for the enemy to gauge the exact position, if his scout or his airman could once locate the limbers and the horses. You

cannot make horses, like men, dig them-selves into the earth, but a friendly piece of bush or wood will help considerably. If it was the gunners' business to come into action, and to deliver effective fire with the greatest rapidity, the driver was responsible for bringing the guns from one position to another in the shortest possible space of time.

A battery changing position under fire did so at some risk. More often than not the necessity for the change was brought about by the fact that the enemy had located the battery's position, and was dropping shells in dangerous proximity. It requires more than ordinary courage to bring your horses up to the gun whilst the enemy's shells are bursting left and right, and to bring those guns out of action by the shortest possible route to safety, much skill and more daring are needed.

Five days a week—sometimes six—the batteries went out for their hard training, and no "bad weather" conditions were allowed to lessen the planned severity of the

daily work. They learnt to know their horses and they learnt to know their guns, and in their knowledge was love as the time went by—love and a whole-hearted professional pride in guns and horses both. A vivid little picture of the return of a Kitchener battery from its day's work comes from Rudyard Kipling's pen :—

"They came in at last far down the park, heralded by that unmistakable half-grumble, half-grunt of guns on the move. The picketed horses heard it first, and one of them neighed long and loud. . . .

"When a battery comes into camp it 'parks' all six guns at the appointed place, side by side in one mathematically straight line, and the accuracy of the alignment is, like ceremonial-drill with the Foot, a fair test of its attainments. The ground was no treat for parking. Specimen trees and draining ditches had to be avoided and cir-cumvented. The gunners, their reins, the guns, the ground, were equally wet, and the slob dropped away like gruel from the brake-shoes. And they were Londoners—clerks,

THE CAVALRYMAN IS NOW INSTRUCTED IN THE USE OF THE BAYONET. – RECRUITS ARE SEEN LEARNING HOW TO USE THEIR NOVEL ARM TO ITS BEST ADVANTAGE.

THE CIVIL SERVICE RECRUITS AT BAYONET EXERCISE IN HYDE PARK.

MULES, WHICH ARE NOW BEING USED FOR GUN TEAMS, ARE PROVERBIALLY OBSTINATE, AS THOSE WHO HAD TO TRAIN THEM QUICKLY FOUND OUT.

"But they were all home and at home in their saddles and seats. They said nothing; their officers said little enough to them. They came in across what had once been turf; wheeled with tight traces; halted, un-hooked; the wise teams stumped off to their pickets, and, behold, the six guns were left precisely where they should have been left to the fraction of an inch. You could see the wind blowing the last few drops of wet from each leather muzzle-cover at exactly the same angle.

mechanics, shop assistants, and delivery men—anything and everything that you please. It was all old known evolutions, taken unconsciously in the course of their day's work by men well abreast of it."

The difficulty of creating 130 new batteries of artillery was great. The guns themselves could be readily cast, but the training of men and officers —especially officers—was a much more complicated business than getting ready the *personnel* of the infantry. In the first six months of the war the chiefs of the R.A. accomplished wonders — how great those wonders were history will testify.

### The Cavalry

GENERALLY speaking, although reserve regiments were formed, and were

IN THE COURSE OF A MIMIC BATTLE. – A MACHINE-GUN OF THE ROYAL BERKS IN POSITION OF A HAY-RICK.

GETTING READY THE HORSES' MEAL: A BUSY SCENE AT THE CHAFF MACHINE.

attached, for the purposes of administration, to existing cavalry regiments, no supreme effort was made to increase largely the force of cavalry at our disposal. Aeroplane and motor-car have greatly minimised the value of this dashing arm; the inventor of barbed-wire has checked its effectiveness in the charge; never again can there be a charge of a Light Brigade nor can we witness decisive actions such as Frederick the Great secured with his famous cavalry; during a long period of the war our cavalry were employed in the trenches as infantrymen.

Our experience was duplicated in the German and French armies, and only Russia was able, during the winter, to utilise her cavalry to fulfil its proper function.

For the cavalry recruit the riding school training was more thorough and more intricate than that which the young artillery-man experienced. The budding cavalry-man was taught to ride with his lance, and to employ that lance. He underwent, too, much of the training which the infantry-man was called upon to endure.

He might still be profitably employed in making sudden raids upon an enemy's flank, but in the warfare which we experienced in the north of France and in Flanders, the enemy's flanks were protected on the one extremity by the sea and on the

other by the Swiss frontier, and there was no opportunity, during the long period of trench war, to use our horsemen for the development of cavalry tactics.

The lessons of the war taught the cavalry that, in addition to their own duties, they must undertake duties which ordinarily were consigned to the infantry. At any moment the campaign might develop so that the employment of cavalry was impossible, and to meet this contingency the new cavalry unit learnt something of trench work, and added to their training a very complete course of trench-digging. The necessity for this had been made apparent in the fourth, fifth, and sixth months of the war, when the cavalry held entrenched lines and beat back the enemy. The 16th Lancers lost the best of their men, and some of the best of their officers, not in the dashing cavalry charges with which their name is historically associated, but in the patient and trying work of the trench line in the region of Ypres. It was a cavalry regiment, the 5th Dragoons, which made a gallant charge on foot and drove the enemy out of their trenches.

Throughout the war cavalry have performed infantry duty without complaint, and without in any way impairing their efficiency as cavalrymen.

Trench warfare, however, was a condition of affairs not likely to last, and whilst the

Government made the training of cavalry a secondary and even a tertiary consideration, men were trained to fill up the gaps in the existing cavalry formation and to act as reserves against the time when the altered conditions of warfare would allow of the employment of this arm.

The cavalryman's day's work began at the same time as the artilleryman's. The trumpet called him to stables with the same regularity, and if he only had one horse to look after, as against the two which the driver of the R.A. had in his charge, it was a different stamp of horse, requiring even more care and attention than the more robust draught horse of the artillery.

## Royal Engineers

If the cavalry had to some extent lost its *raison d'être* because of the scientific developments of the last century, the corps of Royal Engineers had increased in importance from the very causes that had diminished the glories of the cavalry arm, which had touched its zenith in the mistaken but glorious charge of Balaclava.

The Royal Engineers is a title which covers a dozen different services. There is

the field engineer, who constructs bridges and roads, who lays down pontoons and fixes field telephones and telegraphs, who plans and makes trenches and fortifications, who mines bridges and destroys railway lines—and builds them again when an opportune moment arrives. There is the engineer who operates those telephones and telegraphs. There is the engineer who is an expert in explosives; the engineer who can build; the engineer who can only destroy—you might go on to the end of this chapter, dividing and sub-dividing the duties, responsibilities, and qualities of this remarkable corps. Every engine of destruction which science has given to us has been operated in the first case by the Engineers.

The artillery, no less than the infantry, depend very largely upon the engineer's knowledge for their success. The cavalry must work hand in hand with him. The Army Service Corps is dependent upon him, and the Royal Army Medical Corps, before it can set about its merciful work of succouring the wounded and caring for the sick, must first consult the engineering authorities.

TROOPERS CLEANING UP HARNESS IN READINESS FOR AN INSPECTION.

A TARPAULIN RAFT BUILT BY THE 9TH NORTH STAFFORDSHIRE REGIMENT AT HASTINGS. IT IS CARRYING SIXTY-TWO
MEN.

Let us deal first with the young field engineer, the knowledge he is called upon to acquire and the method of his training. He differed very little from the blue-suited infantryman in the early days of his training, and it was only when the earlier stages had passed, and when the infantryman was addressing himself to the business of attack and defence, that the engineer recruit moved by another road to his appointed end. That he had to build bridges, learn the value of strut and stay, acquaint himself with breaking strains, and accomplish wonders with pontoons, huge flat-bottomed boats carried on wagons, we know. The growth of the Boy Scout movement has familiarised us

MEN OF THE ROYAL ENGINEERS BUILDING A PONTOON BRIDGE.

CHILLY WORK – BRIDGE CONSTRUCTION OVER A HALF-FROZEN STREAM.

with the method of building miniature bridges for crossing little streams, and it is not necessary in a work of this character to go into details as to the technical difficulties which the recruit had to overcome. We may dismiss, too, the case of the Royal Engineer "driver," who brought the pontoons and the field telegraphs and the various impedimenta of the corps into action, for his training was very similar to that which has been described in the case of the driver in the Royal Field Artillery.

The engineer recruit must learn as much about artillery as the gunner of that regiment knows. He must add to that a certain technical knowledge which the gun-

A PRACTICAL LESSON IN BRIDGE-BUILDING – EXPLAINING FIRST STEPS TO RECRUITS.

BUILDING A BRIDGE AT BRANKSOME – CARRYING THE PILES TO THE STREAM.

porary character; whilst the floating bridge is that which is laid down, often under fire of the enemy, and is a rough wooden roadway, supported by pontoons (flat-bottomed boats which are carried on wagons), casks, ordinary boats or rafts.

There are other bridges which are intended to cover the gaps in an existing bridge which has been broken at one point. There were certain rough methods of calcu-

ner is not asked to acquire. In the bridge work his knowledge was complete. The fixed bridge, resting on the bottom; the flying bridge; the floating bridge, built on pontoon, cask, boat, or raft, were the A B C of his craft. He must learn to work out the buoyancy of boats or rafts by mathematical calculations. He must know the minimum space for camps, and the most effective cover for artillery.

The bridges which engineers

DRIVING IN THE PILES WITH A MONKEY AND TACKLE.

are called upon to create may be roughly divided into three kinds. The fixed bridge, which rests on the bottom on a trestle or pile. This variety of bridge is one used to replace temporarily important bridges which have been destroyed on the line of march, and its creation is a matter of days and sometimes weeks.

The flying bridge is one of a more tem-

lation which the recruit had to carry in his head. A bridge which would take infantry in fours, crowded, would carry field guns, howitzers, and ordinary wagons. He had to learn when one type of bridge could be used with advantage, when another was wholly unsuitable. If the bottom of a stream could be touched across its entire width, a trestle bridge was the most economical method of bridging. If a float-ing bridge was to be employed, he had to work out its buoyancy in pounds. Bridge building was a science which called into employment all his mathematical know-ledge. All these things the new Royal Engineer had to know.

He learnt, too, the subtle differences between gun-cotton, dynamite, and gun-powder, and had certain tables fixed for him as to the amount of each which might be employed in the demolition of buildings or bridges. To make sure, he was taught to use 50 per cent. more in the face of an enemy than in ordinary circumstances. The exact quantity of gun-cotton to destroy a wall, a pier, an arch, or a girder he committed to memory. None of the grim possibilities of war were left untouched by his instructor.

"If the guns have to be abandoned, destroy them," said the calm engineering officer, discussing the matter with the same placidity as if he were a professor of psycho-logy laying down academic premises. He detailed the correct way of destroying a gun.

"You will load it with shell, pack your gun-cotton charge behind it, and fire. Put two pounds of gun-cotton for a 3-inch gun, and double the charge for every inch of calibre over 3 inches."

Gun-cotton was of no use against wire entanglements, and heavy explosive shells aimed at these obstacles merely made them worse by creating pitfalls under them.

"When you're looking out for fords," his instructor went on, "remember that cavalry want 4 feet and infantry 3 feet. Guns want 2 feet 4 inches."

It was an interesting course, unlike any other in the world, fascinating to the tyro, and destined to be not only immensely helpful to him in his Army career, but to assist him materially in ordering his thoughts when he returned to civilian life. The recruit did not know, until he had been made acquainted with the fact, that if you multiply the breadth, the depth, and the velocity of running water by 9,000, you dis-cover in your sum the gallons that pass in twenty-four hours. If you wanted to secure an idea of the velocity, you had but to throw a floating object into the stream, watch how many feet it drifts in a minute. If it drifts 6, 6 is the velocity figure.

And there was much more that the en-gineer recruit had to learn; to indicate only one or two subjects suggests a rough idea of some of the training which he went through. The breaking strain of rope, the gradient of roads, the tying of knots, the scientific handling of huge bulks, the mathematical precision which attaches to the building of modern fortifications; of these things he must have a working knowledge, and that working knowledge must be instilled into his mind in the first few months of his service.

The Royal Engineers is largely made up of mechanics, and men who possessed any trade were care-fully drafted so that their civilian knowledge might be of the greatest service to the Army. A farrier presenting him-self for enlistment at one of the re-cruiting offices would be very unlikely to find himself in an in-fantry regiment. A working elec-trician with a knowledge of telegraph and telephone instru-ments would also find the letters R.E. attached to his name. It was easier for the pro-verbial camel to

PULLING THE CENTRE SPAN OF A BRIDGE INTO POSITION.

get through the eye of a needle than it was for a trained mechanician to reach the infantry regiments of the Army, unless, of course, he expressed a desire to serve in that capacity.

The telegraphists of the Royal Engineers were strengthened largely by men who were drafted from the General Post Office, and it may be news to many that the experts engaged at Army headquarters were, in the main, men of a great racing staff. In every big post office division there is a movable body of men, who travel from one racecourse to another to deal with the immense amount of telegraphic correspondence which arises out of betting, &c. These comprise some of the most expert workers in the service—men who can handle hundreds of thousands of messages in the shortest time.

he could say with truth that he was qualified to describe himself as a competent "engineer."

There was no limit to the length of a telephone or telegraph wire which the Royal Engineer could lay at a gallop. The wire was carried in big reels and was paid out as the wagon went forward at full gallop. Caught up by the horsemen, and thrown clear of the road, it was fixed with extraordinary rapidity by the men who followed behind, to tree, post, and fence—whichever offered the best advantage. It is seldom necessary to lay more than ten miles of new line in one day, for armies do not progress at any very rapid rate, and temporary "air lines" are only necessary to connect the shifting headquarters of the various staffs. All the time they are

MEN OF THE CYCLIST CORPS AT EPSOM PARADING AFTER A HEAVY FALL OF SNOW.

Though they were not enlisted for Kitchener's Army, and, indeed, came into the strength of the Army department in quite an unusual way, they were valuable additions to the new strength of the Royal Engineers.

The men who could lay telegraph lines at full gallop across a country were necessarily trained in the service, but engineer officers were agreeably surprised to find that, even in this expert work, their new men were able to make almost as good a showing as the more experienced members of the corps. This was part of the training of the Royal Engineer recruit. He concentrated till he became a specialist in his job; he learnt to work swiftly but thoroughly; and there came a time in his training when

operating, other branches of the Royal Engineers are repairing the main lines which are usually operated in time of peace, and can be easily put in working order providing the destructive enemy has left the posts standing.

There was no shortage of instructors. The great engineers of England, the architects, the master minds who create towns, the brilliant railroad workers who have laid their lines across the wastes of Africa and South America, the builders of bridges, the diggers of wells in arid places—all these came forward to offer their assistance to the overworked headquarters' staff, and by lecture, example, and personal tuition, succeeded in developing the raw material.

THE 10TH SERVICE BATTALION OF THE ROYAL WARWICKSHIRE REGIMENT AT SIGNALLING INSTRUCTION.

The recruiting officers found the trades unions of Great Britain of invaluable assistance. A man might describe himself as a bricklayer or as an engineer, as a farrier or a forge hand, in a light-hearted moment, when he was no more than a labourer or an assistant to the skilled workers of these trades. A trade union card, however, solved all difficulties, and the trade union card, properly attested, brought men into the engineers to a rate of pay much higher than they could have enjoyed in an infantry regiment. Britannia was no niggard in point of payment. She paid fair wages to all, and offered the young mechanical student privileges which he could not have secured in civilian life. She took the technical students from the schools and put them in the Flying Corps, to nurse the motors and to assist in the work of reconstruction. She took a large number of these for the R.E., and gave them no cause, even from the sordid point of view of wage-earning, to regret that they had taken the step which made them Army men.

Men with a knowledge of telegraphy were made welcome. The hundreds of young men who made wireless telegraphy their hobby, Britannia found instant employment for. The Royal Engineers, with their portable masts and their flying aerials, furnished the Army with this means of communication.

Though not actually attached to the Royal Engineers, one of the new Kitchener battalions of infantry was specially designed to render valuable assistance to R.E. in preparing their field fortifications. This was a navvies' battalion, to which Mr. Ward, the Labour leader, and Member of Parliament, was appointed as Captain. Mr. Ward himself, in his younger days, had been a soldier and had fought in the Egyptian campaign, and his position as head of the Navvies' Union made his new appointment of peculiar value.

A MOTOR-CYCLIST AT SEMAPHORE PRACTICE.

The Navvies' Battalion was made up of those brawny men, the hardest-muscled of our citizens, who are engaged in peace time upon road construction, the rough work of building railways, bridges, etc. Many of these men were much older than the average soldier, but the British navvy is accounted quite good at fifty. As trench and fortification builders, the Navvies' Battalion was an invaluable acquisition to the British Army, and the man who first had the idea of its formation deserves much credit.

Even as the new units of the Artillery could talk with pride of the work of their corps in the field, so might the young engineer speak of the work which the Royal Engineers had accomplished during the present war. The annals of the corps are filled with incidents of unselfish devotion to duty.

The officer who was shot dead after making three attempts, and the last successful, to destroy a bridge under the enemy's fire; the sapper who continued, though wounded, in repairing a barbed-wire entanglement under heavy fire; the heroic corporal who destroyed yet another bridge though shot at close range—these are only typical instances where the men of the corps have shown a total oblivion to danger in the performance of their duties.

The "Kitchener Engineer" learnt much on parade ground and workshop, but he imbibed the spirit of the corps from the daily example which the "old" Engineers were setting him.

VISUAL TRAINING – THE MEN HAVE TO DISCOVER A SUPPOSED GERMAN MACHINE-GUN WHICH IS MARKED ON THE MAP.

UNIVERSITY AND PUBLIC SCHOOLS AMBULANCE CORPS ON A FIELD DAY AT EPSOM.

## CHAPTER V

### THE TRAINING OF THE R.A.M.C. RECRUITS.—ARMY SERVICE CORPS.— THE NAVAL BRIGADE.

Amongst the first to answer the call of Lord Kitchener for men were the young students from St. Bartholomew's, St. Thomas's, Guy's Hospital, and all the other great hospitals throughout the country, young men whose medical education was not yet completed, but whose experience and knowledge were most valuable for the work for which they gladly volunteered, viz., that of the Royal Army Medical Corps. These young men were quickly drafted to the new medical formations grouped about the great military hospitals at Aldershot, Woolwich, Netley, Portsmouth, York, Dublin, and Edinburgh. Aldershot was naturally the most important of these training centres, for this is the administrative heart of the Medical Service.

Possibly the standard of the Royal Army Medical Corps was never so high as it was in the six months following the outbreak of war, for a large proportion of the new accessions to its ranks was made up of young medical students, who came straight from the hospitals to give their services to the New Army.

Although the short musketry service was dispensed with (since, at any rate theoretically, we were fighting a civilised nation, and the musketry course was only included

with a view to the R.A.M.C. man's self-protection when Britain was engaged in war with savage tribes), the new R.A.M.C. recruit went through very much the same training as the infantry soldier.

At first his training was designed to fit him to deal effectively and immediately with wounded cases in the field.

He learnt stretcher drill, arranged to familiarise him with the carriage of wounded. He was taught how to lift and carry the sick and maimed, how to break step so that there was no unevenness of motion, and how to move expeditiously with his stretcher to the point where he was required.

He attended many classes, where he was lectured on the various physical parts of the wonderful and complicated human body.

The lectures were not chosen haphazard or at the whim of the instructors, but followed a course laid down in the R.A.M.C. manual. The theories of nursing were thoroughly discussed. A rough outline of physiology, including the location of bones and important arteries, was given by surgical lecturers.

"The Manual of the Royal Army Medical Corps" gave the awe-stricken recruit some idea of his responsibilities. He was told there that he was responsible in peace and in war for the nursing of the sick, the dispensing of medicines, charge of equipment, making requisitions for fuel, light, provisions, and all supplies and repairs, the cooking and expenditure of diets, the custody of patients' kits, the cleanliness of the hospital and its surroundings, and for bedding, linen, and clothing.

When he made acquaintance with the Army regulation stretcher he learnt some very useful things.

"There are forty-six ways of lifting a wounded man," said the cynical officer, directing one stretcher squad at Aldershot, "and forty-five of them are wrong. The only right way of lifting the wounded is the one I am teaching you now. It has never been improved upon, and I have no great hope that you will succeed where the Medical Council has failed."

One man at each end of the stretcher, with a leather sling over his shoulders, the loops at the end supporting the handles of the stretcher poles, and a man on each side rendering what support they could by grasping the poles in the centre, made a stretcher party. The two bearers must not

walk "left, right, left," and they were taught that the step advocated in a popular song offered less distress to the wounded occupant. In other words, they were told to "shuffle along."

For several days in succession I watched the drilling of the stretcher squad go forward on the barrack square. Some of the men were told off to act as wounded soldiers, grinning a little uneasily at first as they read the injuries they were supposed to have suffered, neatly detailed on

A WOUNDED MAN BEING BROUGHT IN, SUPPORTED ON TWO RIFLES PLACED BETWEEN A COUPLE OF BICYCLES.

THE 1ST SOUTH MIDLAND MOUNTED BRIGADE FIELD AMBULANCE PRACTISING 'THE FIREMAN'S LIFT'.

cards attached to the buttons of their jackets.

Then, under the critically watchful eye of a corporal, four recruits would render first aid to the "specimen case," in accordance with the injuries described on the label. Once again there was dinned into their ears the only proper way of lifting the "sufferer" on to the stretcher.

"Under no circumstances," reiterated the instructor, "must you lift a wounded man by his arms; you must not drag him into any uncomfortable position in order to save the stretcher bearers a little extra exertion. The wounded part itself—particularly if a bone is affected—must be grasped firmly by one of the bearers while the lifting process is going on."

And in other spheres of his work, the recruit was taught there was only one way to do things—the "Army way," long-proven to be the best. The R.A.M.C. man learnt the most effective methods of stopping bleeding, of applying splints, bandages, and dressings.

The voice of the instructor came again, telling him that quick action and efficiency must mark all that he did.

"Every soldier going into action carries a field dressing, consisting of a triangular bandage, safety-pins, and antiseptic dress-

HOW A SOLIDER IS REMOVED FROM THE BATTLEFIELD. HIS WOUNDS ARE BANDAGED, AND HE IS THEN SECURELY STRAPPED ON TO THE HORSE.

NO. 2 FIELD AMBULANCE OF THE ROYAL ARMY MEDICAL CORPS ON PARADE.

A R.A.M.C. HOSPITAL IN THE FIELD, SHOWING THE KITCHEN AND COOKING FACILITIES.

TRANSFERRING THE STRETCHER INTO AN AMBULANCE WAGON.

ing, stitched in a small package inside his coat. When you find a wounded soldier on the field, tear out the dressing from his coat and give him such rough first-aid as is possible under the circumstances."

This of course can only be done on the field of battle itself, and the rough treatment would be replaced, at the first collecting station, with a more thorough examination of the wound and the application of more scientific methods for preventing infection.

Lessons in more elaborate detail were given in the art of dressing the injured, but these generally took place in "class"— a room set aside for the purpose, in which the recruits were lectured morning and afternoon by competent instructors.

Stretcher drill and "class" occupied three months of the recruit's time, at the end of which he knew that the sub-clavian artery was not to be confused with the thoracic aorta. He knew the whole art of bandaging. He knew the spica twist, the reverse spiral, and the bandaging movement for clavical fractures. He had arrived at a point of knowledge where the sight of a granny knot made him all but swoon, and he could take drowned and apparently dead people and bring them back to life.

Now he was drafted to a hospital, and came actually into touch with the sick; he learnt by experience to prepare a patient for operation and take a temperature or change a sheet.

He is now a "third-class orderly," but by dint of working hard and showing his doctor that he understood his business, he would very soon earn the first grade of efficiency and become a second-class orderly, the badge for which is a thin red cord about the forearm. When I say red I should, of course, have said a dull maroon, those being the facings of the corps. (Officially they are "cherry," but nobody ever saw a cherry of the colour the Royal Army Medical Corps wear.) The highest grade is that of "first-class orderly," a distinction not so commonly granted nowadays.

Few people realise the extraordinary care which the Army displays towards its sick and its wounded. You never hear a wounded man speak of the R.A.M.C. except in terms of the highest praise of the Corps, and it was a knowledge of the responsibilities attaching to their work that made the Kitchener section of the Royal Army Medical Corps display fine zeal, unfailing industry, and splendid courage.

The war speedily took a heavy toll of the R.A.M.C. Constant drafts of new

Kitchener men were necessary to replace the gallant members of the Corps who fell in the execution of their duty. That one officer of the Corps (Captain Martin Leake) should have won the Victoria Cross twice is a fine tribute to the courage and the endurance of a body whose motto is "Faithful in Labour."

No Corps in the field to-day has more arduous or dangerous work than the R.A.M.C.

Night or day, in battle or lull of battle, the orderly of the Royal Army Medical Corps is working desperately to relieve the sufferings of the men who have "caught it" on the day of battle. All day long while the battle is raging and the trenches are spitting fire the little stretcher squads are crouching, awaiting their work. A man is down, and, stooping low, the squad go swiftly to his side. A glance is almost enough to tell the corporal in charge the nature of the injury. A doctor is there and makes a rough examination. And all the time the kneeling figures beside the prostrate man are a mark for the bullets that sweep across the field. The injury is diagnosed, the first dressing is applied. Deft and skilful hands lift the man to the stretcher, and the Red Cross men carry him to where, somewhere under cover, an ambulance wagon is waiting.

Further in the rear, away from the range of the guns, is a field hospital, where the injury will be examined with greater care, the limb set if it is necessary to set it, and the larger and more elaborate dressing arranged. Here, too, it may be possible to keep the patient for a day or so if there is any

danger in moving him. In one large, light tent the surgeons, enveloped in their white coats, or bare-armed, are operating where immediate operations are necessary. Behind the surgeon, ready now with the knife that he wants, now with a needle or ligature or forceps, is the operating orderly.

So near the Front you will not see a woman. It is the man of the Royal Army Medical Corps who does the work—the big, quick, dangerous work. The picturesque nurse, gentle of hand, will come later when the long hospital train has reached the base hospital. It is the orderly who is the first man to be smitten, the orderly who keeps his silent vigil throughout the night by the dying on the field, the orderly who superintends the last sad rites of all.

The women, too, have done their splendid share. One would like to call them "Kitchener nurses"; and, so far as they enlisted for the duration of the war only, this description is an accurate one. The British Red Cross Society, which co-operated with the R.A.M.C. throughout the war, and

'FIRST AID.' — WITH THE U.P.S. AMBULANCE CORPS AT EPSOM.

ARMY COOKS BEING GIVEN INSTRUCTION AT THE COOKERY SCHOOL.

collected through *The Times* newspaper £1,000,000 for motor ambulances, hospitals, and the general relief of the sick, produced its own staff and its own hospitals, which were augmented by private enterprise, notably in the case of Millicent, Duchess of Sutherland, and of other patriotic ladies, who put aside their society duties, and braved the discomforts of the field.

### Army Service Corps

It took me a long time to learn all I wanted to know about the Kitchener Army Service Corps—what manner of men they were, what callings they had forsaken for the new life of great endeavour, how they liked it and what it was they were doing. The variety of work that falls to be done by this great handmaid of the fighting line is immense. The growth of the new army, reaching such proportions as it did, added enormously to the work of the Army Service Corps. Not only were new arrangements to be made and the already wide organisation of the Corps considerably extended, but the training of the new instruments of supply were to tax the capacity of these men to the utmost.

The duties that fall to the Army Service Corps are multifarious. They are the general servants of the Army. They are

more than this; they are the cooks, the housemaids, the carpenters, the blacksmiths, saddlers, the general provision stores, and they have in addition the charge of everything that has to do with transport —an immense business in itself. Upon their work more than upon any other department of Army life, depend the comfort and well-being of the troops. In some respects the Army Service Corps resembles the Royal Engineers, in that it is a designation which embraces a multitude of varying activities. The mud-stained driver who urges his weary horses along the sodden roads of Flanders, the spectacled clerk in his tin hut at the base working out "indents" and tabulating requisitions, the expert who deals with the storing and distribution of petrol, the motor-car lorry driver, the wheelwright, the shoeing smith, the food expert, and often the creator of emergency time-tables, were all members of the Corps.

The first new recruits to the Army Service Corps, the men who enlisted at the outbreak of war, were swiftly, without any military training whatever, bundled off to the front.

"There was no time to teach them the goose step," said an Army Service Corps colonel grimly; "the new men had half an hour's straight talk with their captain. They were told the things they must do and the things that were forbidden, given a khaki suit, and rushed off to France."

Though they were enlisted for the duration of the war only, they cannot be exactly described as members of Kitchener's Army. The recruits who followed on, who came flocking to Woolwich and Aldershot on Lord Kitchener's appeal, had a more specific training. But it was a training which ran concurrently with the performance of useful work. The transport recruit, that is to say, the man who had to deal with horses, had to be taught to ride, and, in addition, to drive. The driving tuition offered very little difficulty, because the majority of the men who went into the Army Service Corps had had plenty of experience in directing their four-footed charges through the maze of town traffic. And even the riding presented only half the terrors which it did to men who were wholly unaccustomed to horses.

The military authorities left nothing to chance. A man might be described as a driver, but he had to prove his ability before he was allowed to take a wagon out on the road. He was exercised in driving between "dolls," and was tutored in the art of bringing his wagon into line. Only light wagons are driven. The heavier vehicles are drawn by four or more horses, ridden in the same way as the artillery horses are ridden, by postillions. However far his other military training may have advanced, he was no sooner proficient in riding and driving than he was put to actual work, to the conveyance of supplies from stores to ship or from ship to stores, the bringing of ammunition from arsenal to magazine, and was made generally acquainted with the elementary business of distribution.

In truth, he had very little time for exercise in arms. He performed his simple drill, he learned the use and the employment of a rifle, he marched and countermarched and performed simple military evolutions, and fired his recruit's course at the ranges. But his most important duties were quite unassociated with attack and defence, and upon the efficient performance of these duties his attention was concentrated.

The motor-bus drivers, the chauffeurs, the mechanics and the workmen of skilled trades, and the thousands of men from dockyards, railways, and such like industries, who rushed to swell the ranks, were in time duly sorted out. The new supply men fell into their positions naturally. They were chosen for their particular jobs by reason of their civil occupations. The bakers and the butchers were apportioned their departments; the clerks and the typists were sent to the innumerable offices; many others

THE MAKING OF AN ARMY COOK – ABOUT A DOZEN MEN ARE TAKEN FROM EACH REGIMENT AND TRAINED IN THE CULINARY ART.

found instant employment with the skilled men who handle the leather work, harness, etc., of the Army; whilst men of a score of trades who could contribute to the efficiency of the Army Service Corps were immediately drafted to positions which enabled them to give their best to the service.

Yet, however good a man might be in his own trade, he was to learn that there was a special Army way of doing things, and it was necessary for those who had to deal with the supply of foodstuffs to learn many new lessons. In the field there are no giant bakehouses where bread can be prepared under the most hygienic con-

taught me something. I think, when I have finished my training, I shall start a field bakery to supply old soldiers with the kind of bread they are familiar with."

The dough which is mixed and kneaded in the open field must be well protected against infection; the water must be carefully examined, and, if possible, filtered; most elaborate precautions must be taken against contamination from the air.

"Making Army Service Corps bread," said an officer, "is more a ritual than an operation."

The methods by which the rations are prepared by the regimental cook were

HOT MEALS ON THE MARCH. – ONE OF THE FIELD KITCHENS WHICH SUPPLY THE ARMY'S WANTS.

ditions. The Army must create not only its food but the conditions under which it is prepared. Steam and electric bakeries are, of course, replaced by roughly-made but efficacious field ovens, and the baker must learn to build these, and not only build them, but keep them in such repair as would enable the best results to be secured. I have seen these improvised bakeries in course of construction, and have been amazed alike by the thoroughness of the training and by the perfection of the field ovens.

"I thought I knew all about baking," said a recruit ruefully, "but the Army has

strange to most of the men. There are two methods in particular which the cooks have to be trained to follow. The men were taught to perform the work under the conditions which they would experience at the Front. Under war conditions, much of the food is cooked by stewing in kettles in a field kitchen. The arrangements depend upon the length of time the troops are likely to remain at the particular place. If the stay was only the matter of a night the kettles were simply placed on the ground in two parallel rows, with another row of kettles resting crosswise on the top of these, the fire being laid underneath the top row and

ARMY TRANSPORT DRIVING THROUGH A WATER-SPLASH.

between the first two rows of kettles, a very simple but effective method. Another quick way, particularly when loose bricks are available, is to build two rough walls between which the fire is made up, the kettles being placed along the top. The more permanent form of field kitchen consists of shallow trenches, which are built of stones, sods or clay.

At the Front in the field of war these

UNLOADING FORAGE FOR THE HORSES.

WITH THE ARMY SERVICE CORPS – A TRANSPORT TRAIN, PARKED BESIDE THE ROAD DURING AN ADVANCE.

kitchens had to be built on a much more extensive scale—often preparing food for 800 to 1,000 men. By a system of shallow trenches, covered in with roofs converging into one chimney, the inside of these kitchen trenches would be plastered with clay, and, as a rule, they would be roofed in. Whenever possible, bread is baked in the improvised field ovens once a day, generally shortly after sunrise. This baking is served for breakfast, and during the day for dinner and tea. As evidence of the ingenuity of soldiers, it may be mentioned that when in the field, beer-barrels are often converted into serviceable ovens. All that

is necessary is to set a beer-barrel upright in a trench and knock out one end. The interior is then filled with fuel, and the top and sides are thickly covered with clay. When the fire is lit the woodwork of the barrel burns away, leaving the clay, which is held together by the iron bands, in the form of a shell, which thus forms the oven.

There is quite a contingent of Army butchers in the field. To obtain fresh meat cattle must be purchased and killed on the spot. A squad consisting of six men will kill and dress two bullocks in 45 minutes, or prepare three sheep for roasting in 12 minutes. Thus, in a working day of eight

MOTOR LORRY USED AS A REPAIR SHOP.

hours, a squad will kill and dress 20 bullocks or 120 sheep. It is calculated that one butcher is required for every 1,000 men.

The immense quantities of meat required for the Army in the field were procured either through open buying in the market or through contractors. Large quantities were bought and shipped by Government agents, and here a special branch of the Royal Army Medical Corps, a branch of that "Sanitary Corps" which is a sort of Medical-Army-Service-Royal-Engineer department rolled into one, tested every scrap of meat for signs of disease before it was passed for the troops. It may be said that contractors supplying what is popularly known as bad meat are very often innocent agents. The meat, which is frozen and sent to England, may arrive fresh and sound and be handed over to the military authorities, who, if they delay issuing it for a single day, may find the beef "sweating." To obviate this danger, not only on behalf of the Army but on behalf of the contractor, second and sometimes third examinations were made, and a final inspection was given to the meat in the store of the unit to which it was consigned.

The catering men of the new Army were never idle, thousands of men had to be fed, and fed to time, coming in from their drill or from manoeuvres in the field, often soaked with the rain and bespattered with mud; they looked for a hot meal, and it required

CATERPILLAR TRACTION-ENGINE USED BY THE ARMY FOR DRAWING HEAVY GUNS.

WHEN GUNS ARE ENTRAINED THEY ARE STOWED VERY CLOSELY UPON THE TRUCKS.

ARMY FARRIERS AT WORK.

gigantic work and organisation to feed more than a million men.

The war brought an enormous strain upon one other department, viz., that of the mechanical transport. Well supplied as the Army was with motor wagons for use in time of peace, its equipment in this respect totalled only a very small percentage of its ultimate requirements. A subsidy scheme had been in operation for a year or two by means of which the Government had a call on a large number of cars and motor-lorries of approved type belonging to private individuals. But these were insufficient to meet the needs of this unexampled war. The Government made rapid search, commandeered all the likely motor-buses and taxi-cabs, called to its aid the industries which employed motor-lorries, and almost in the twinkling of an eye had created a new transport service four or five times the normal size of the Army Service Corps Motor Traction Department in days of peace. Men had to be quickly found to run this fleet of motors, and they were soon forthcoming. Journeying to and fro I conversed with many of these men cheerfully working like slaves at their new jobs. In the drill sheds I listened to discussions on the virtues, or the infirmities, of this or that car or lorry. Here a man would be wrestling with an evil-smelling engine, or a disordered clutch or gear-box. A Thornycroft would be getting

thing you learn in London is any good at the Front. You have to learn to drive on the edge of a knife, and go through roads that you can bail out with a bucket.

"This isn't all. The Tommies we carried out there persisted in roasting and chaffing us unmercifully when we stuck. They got down and looked at the 'bus disgustedly."

"'How long are we going to wait here?' said a chap one day.

"'Oh, about an hour—until the repair car comes up,' I told him.

"There was a howl of dismay.

SMITHS AT THE FORGE.

a brand new coat of paint. Another man would be testing the chains; yet another engaged in mysterious operations which necessitated his disappearance into the very heart of the mechanism.

"I'm a motor-'bus driver," said one grimy individual to me; "three months ago I was driving a Cricklewood 'bus without any more idea of war than I could get from the morning papers. I've been out to France, and was brought back to teach the new hands things I'd learned there. Already I feel an old soldier—been under fire too, an' had one 'bus shelled from under me! No-

"'You've got to get busy,' said another fellow, ' or we'll take the Tube.'"

It is this chaffing, these threats to "take another 'bus," which supplied the lighter side of the motor-driver's life at the Front.

"You've no idea of the fun these fellows get out of things. I've seen men come in dog-tired from the trenches, and no sooner were they on the 'bus being driven to some part of the line where they were wanted in reserve than the joke would begin."

A self-appointed conductor would find the man who had only just arrived, and would collect his fare with due solemnity.

THE 63RD FIELD COMPANY, ROYAL ENGINEERS, BUILT THE TRESTLE BRIDGE SHOWN ABOVE ENTIRELY WITH TIMBER THEY CUT FROM THE WOODS.

"They made their own route up, and a favourite one for the conductor to shout was 'Bank, Marble Arch, Wipers, Calais, and the Aisne.'"

Such stories as these, feeble jests as they were, were popular enough with the newly-joined members of the motor transport service. It seemed to stir their imagination and made them keen to share the experience of the "old soldiers" of the corps, and they looked forward as eagerly as any to the day when the order would come to start off for service in France.

The motor transport service was a triumph of skill and organisation. One day I watched the manœuvring of a motor vehicle road train. It was a railway station depôt. A train of motor road vehicles arrived and marshalled up on one side of the road; the vehicles swung round singly or in sections

to a position beside the railway cars. The men handed out the packages, others loaded up. As fast as the motor vehicles were loaded they drew away to form a second line. When the whole road train had received its full complement of supplies the "make-up" of the train was completed, and off they went; everything was complete, down to the last ounce of salt, for the regiments which had to be supplied. My friend the ex-motor-'bus driver added a few hints; at the Front, I gathered, the routine was as follows: In advance of the train a motor-cyclist was despatched, and he kept a certain defined distance ahead. As a rule he was accompanied by a guide, that is, one who knew the roads of the strange country in which the train found itself. The cyclist was sent ahead to see that the road was clear and free from obstructions. Should he come across a hole caused by a "Jack Johnson," which was impassable and could not be avoided, he returned to the officer in charge of the train, who held up the movement, that an alternative road might be chosen. As a rule, owing to the carefulness of the patrol the safety of the road was ascertained before the train left its base. The train was run with machine-like precision. Each vehicle was spaced 20 ft. apart. The speed was severely controlled—the maximum being 12 miles an hour. Now and again the driver, especially the driver of the leading vehicle, was unable to suppress his inclinations for a joy-ride, and would put on a spurt, and if he was left to his own initiative he would at times increase the speed of the train to 18—20 miles an hour; but when one bears in mind the rough pave of the French roads it does not require a very vivid imagination to picture the rolling and swaying of the ungainly vehicle, which was often piled with goods to a maximum height. The result was that the officer in charge of the train maintained a sharp vigilance, and suppressed joy-riding with a stern hand—a restriction, by the way, which was needed. Upon reaching the camp the whole of the vehicles discharged their contents and pulled away ready for the next run.

This being the first war in which mechanical transport (other than steam) had been used, the training of this section of Kitchener's Army had necessarily to be based upon actual experience gained in France. The instructors were men who had passed through several months' hard duty at the Front, and had been carefully selected for their ability to keep their motor going, reducing repairs and breakdowns to a minimum, and establishing their capability to effect serious repairs with speed. Each road train included two travelling workshops, where roadside repairs might be effected, but heavy repairs and general overhauling were carried out either at the camp or at the base as opportunity permitted.

The routine comprises the carrying by mechanical transport of both commissariat and ammunition, which is divided into two

OFFICERS OF THE ARMY SERVICES CORPS, SUPPLY RESERVE DEPOT, DEPTFORD.

distinct sections. I was informed that each division comprises 320 motor vehicles divided into two trains each of 160 cars. For the most part these are vehicles of the heavy type, such as motor lorries of 5 tons capacity. The supply of ammunition and commissariat is carried out every day, and the principle is as follows:—

The officer in charge of the mechanical transport receives indication of the nearest railway station from which the supplies can be transferred. This distance varies;

to-day it may be 15 miles, to-morrow it may be 30. The Commanding Officer, however, knowing the speed possibilities of his train, can gauge how many miles he can cover in the time allotted. The railway station varies also. To-day it may be a big terminus or junction possessed of miles of sidings; but to-morrow it may be just an ordinary village station with only one short siding, but in each case the procedure is the same.

It is not easy for the ordinary civilian to

realise how tremendous is the task of satisfying the myriad needs of an army such as we have now in the field.

An official descriptive despatch gave a staggering glimpse of the mammoth supplies that our Army in France and Belgium swallowed up. The vastness of the work of maintaining the Army may be gauged from a few figures.

In one month there were issued to the troops:—450 miles of telephone wire; 570 telephones; 534,000 sandbags; 10,000 lb. of dubbin for boots; 38,000 bars of soap; 150,000 pairs of socks, and 100,000 pairs of boots. In ten days the number of fur waistcoats given out amounted to 118,160, while during the same period 315,075 flannel belts were distributed. The way that insignificant items mount up where large numbers of men are concerned is shown by the fact that the weight of the average weekly issue of vaseline for the feet is five tons, and that of horseshoes 100 tons.

The same despatch touched on the far-ranging variety of articles needed for different branches of the service. Broadly speaking, it told us, the Ordnance Department supplies the Army with all the clothing, equipment, arms, ammunition, tools, appliances, machinery, and expendable material that can be required, from guns weighing many tons to tin-tacks. In a word, it is the Military Universal Provider.

Some idea of the complexity of one side of the work of the Army Service Corps can be gathered by reference to the official "Vocabulary of Stores," which corresponds to the price-list of a large shop, and contains 50,000 separate items. Stocks of 50,000 different articles have to be procured, transported, stored, and issued to the soldiers in the field!

The war brought to the colours men from every station of life, and it is a notable fact, which I have verified from a dozen different authoritative sources, that whereas the young men of England who were drawn from the better or the middle classes were content and indeed desirous of being included in the infantry masses which were

IN HAVERSACK

EQUIPMENT

IN FULL FIGHTING ORDER AND EQUIPPED FOR EVERY EMERGENCY – THE BRITISH SOLDIER'S BURDEN IN THE FIRING-LINE PICTURED FROM A TO Z. THIS GRAPHIC PORTRAYAL OF EVERYTHING AN INFANTRYMAN CARRIES ON ACTIVE SERVICE WILL ASTONISH MANY WHO HAVE ONLY A VAGUE IDEA OF THE QUANTITY OF ARTICLES INCLUDED IN THE EQUIPMENT OF A SOLDIER OF THE LINE. THE WINTER GOATSKIN JACKET SERVED OUT TO OUR TROOPS IS AN ADDITIONAL ITEM, AND SOMETIMES HE CARRIES ALSO EXTRA RATIONS AND FUEL. (COPYRIGHT, ILLUSTRATED LONDON NEWS)

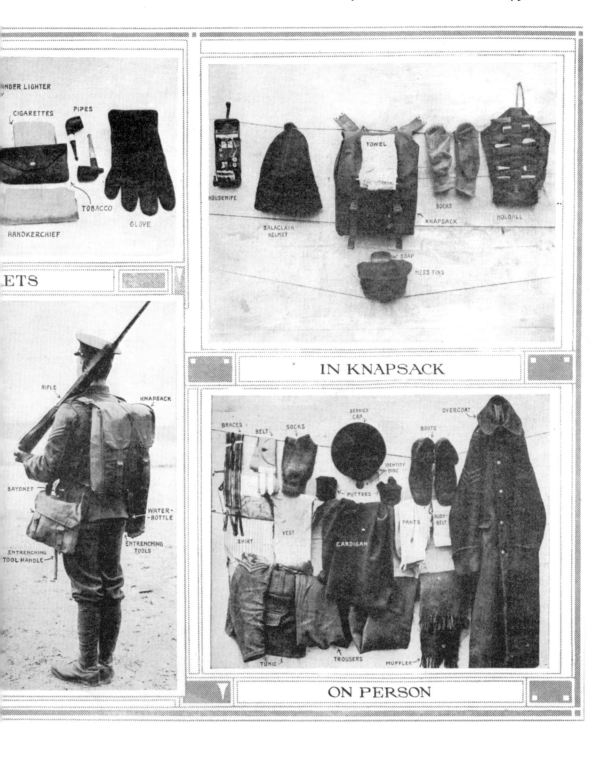

IN KNAPSACK

ON PERSON

FULLY TRAINED MEN OF KITCHENER'S ARMY READY FOR THE FRONT.

forming, men of the labour class had very definite views as to the branch of the service in which their working knowledge would be of the greatest advantage to the Army. In one of the southern depôts, in the course of my tour, a new recruit, a man of 35, came up to see the commanding officer with whom I was speaking. He had a genuine grievance.

"I asked to be put in the Army Service Corps, and I find they've put me into a line regiment," he said.

"Why do you want to go into the Army Service Corps?" asked the Colonel.

"Because I understand the work," was the startling claim.

He had been a carman in the employment of a great London firm of carriers, and in addition to his driving ability he was a good manager of horses, as a written testimonial which he produced to clinch his argument confirmed.

I have said before that skilled labourers found some difficulty in reaching the ranks of the fighting units. Unless they expressed a preference to take their place in the ranks of the battalions, the Army, ever keen on placing men to the best advantage, took the young enthusiasts who came forward at the call of duty, and if they were indubitable artisans, drafted them to the units which could best offer them employment. In the Army Service Corps and Ordnance Corps it was always possible to find openings for the man who knew any kind of trade, and even for the clerk and the typist. It is within my knowledge that five men went to Woolwich to enlist in September. They were not very great friends, but they came from the same locality, and knew one another well enough to pass the time of day, and they decided to make a little party up and go to Woolwich and offer their services *en bloc*. One was a confectioner and baker, one was a mason, two were employed by a large mineral water manufacturer in van delivery, and one was a metal turner. The five were

drafted to five different arms: the bricklayer to the Royal Engineers, one of the carmen to the field artillery, one to the cavalry, whilst the baker went to the Army Service Corps as a matter of course. The metal turner was asked to produce his credentials in proof of his statement that he had been employed in this capacity, and when these were offered and his claim had had practical test he was drafted to the Army Ordnance Corps.

The Ordnance Corps differed from the Army Service Corps and the Royal Engineers in that it was a highly specialised department. It had no room save for the skilled workman in certain particular trades. The Army Ordnance Corps deals with the guns, and, generally speaking, with all the lethal weapons with which the Army is equipped. In addition, in peace time it has charge of certain equipment which cannot by any stretch of imagination be described as warlike. These new men who came into the Ordnance Corps at the moment of crisis found themselves called upon to handle an armament undreamed of in days of peace. The earlier stages of the war had shown the Allies the extraordinary superiority in point of numbers of the enemy's artillery.

Here was the greatest of all the dangers to the Allies, and the nations of the Allies set to work in desperate haste to remedy the deficiency. It is not permissible to tell the number of guns which British arsenals and factories turned out for the use of our Allies, but it is

SCOUTING INSTRUCTION – A MODEL OF THE SEAT OF WAR MADE IN SAND SHOWS RIVERS, RAILWAYS, HILLS, WOODS, CHURCHES, AND OTHER LANDMARKS. AN OFFICER IS INSTRUCTING HIS SQUAD IN THE CORRECT METHOD OF DISCOVERING THE ENEMY'S STRENGTH.

THE WORK OF LAYING THE MONSTER PIECES OF ARTILLERY IS A STRENUOUS BUSINESS, BUT THE BRITISH GUNNERS ARE PRE-EMINENT IN GETTING THEIR HEAVY GUNS INTO POSITION IN THE SHORTEST POSSIBLE TIME.

sufficient to say that from Woolwich to Elswick the factories worked day and night to supply the needs of the armies. The glare of great furnaces lit the midnight skies; the thunder of steam hammers, the roar of whirling wheels, and the throb of tireless engines sounded throughout the land, as howitzer, field gun, and rifle were cast, turned, rifled, and handed over to the growing little army of Ordnance men for distribution to the troops.

Our shortage of guns in the early part of the war was a very serious handicap, and one for which the Ordnance Department was in no way responsible. We had not foreseen a war of such dimensions, and the preparations which were eventually made would never have been sanctioned in time of peace. Right well did the workmen of

England labour to remedy the mischief, and to these men, whose unceasing efforts produced in a miraculously short space of time a great new armament, the thanks of Britain are due.

The Army Ordnance Corps found itself stocking undreamed-of weapons of war. It was responsible for the purchase of great stocks of motor-cycles, and for the issuing of "side-car Maxims" to the new Forces. The head of the department is known as the Master General of Ordnance—a quaint title, which has come down unaltered for a hundred years, and upon him and his men rested a very heavy responsibility.

The Army Ordnance Corps works in the dark, away from the shining light of publicity. The names of its members seldom appear in the casualty lists, and there is no

opportunity in the field for gaining the recognition which is reserved to the executive branches of the Army. Nevertheless, the men of the Corps played their part excellently well. They took their place in the field and acted as gun doctors, renovating, repairing, and nursing the sick cannons back to efficiency. Those men of Kitchener's Army who found themselves in the Ordnance workshops at home and abroad have much indeed to be proud of.

### The Naval Brigade

There began in August the formation of a force which perhaps cannot be rightly included in Kitchener's Army save that a number enjoyed the unique experience of engaging in warfare in the earliest days of their service. Though they were not Army men, they enlisted for service in the Naval Brigade on the same terms as those accepted by Kitchener's Army. The Naval Reserve recruit began and carried out his training under exactly the same conditions as those which the Kitchener Army recruit experienced. If he handled his own field gun and substituted man haulage for the indispensable horse, and if he learned something of the eccentricities of big guns, it was because his system of training was very largely modelled upon the training which the naval recruit receives in barracks.

The naval brigades were housed at the Crystal Palace, and this big glass building, with which every boy and girl of the Empire is acquainted, and which has so often echoed to the myriad feet of football enthusiasts, made perhaps the most wonderful barracks that Great Britain has ever possessed. The spacious grounds and their extraordinary conformation were of invaluable assistance to those charged with the instruction of this great force. Here you had tiny hills, good-sized lakes, wooded country, and stretching away to the far horizon an expanse of valley and low hills to test the judgment and the eyesight of the recruit.

A portion of this force had, as I say, been employed in the defence of Antwerp, and it is not too much to claim that the day or two days which they gained by their defence of the outer lines of that fortress town assisted materially the withdrawal of the Belgian Army to safety. It was a Brigade which found instant favour with the middle-class youth of this country, and it numbered amongst its members artists and distinguished men of letters.

In the hands of the Naval Brigade was the defence of London against hostile aircraft, and every night saw the white beams of their great searchlights sweeping the clouds whilst naval gunners stood by the side of their loaded guns.

### The Miracle Completed

At length the day came; the new Army was in being; it was a hard fact. Drilled, clothed, equipped, the first battalions were ready to take the field in real earnest, and without parade or ostentation were shipped across the Channel. Over a million men, who six months previously had been working at their respective trades, carrying on their businesses in

AT LEAMINGTON THE SOLDIERS' HORSES WERE QUARTERED IN THE STREET, AS THERE WAS NOT SUFFICIENT SUITABLE STABLING IN THE TOWN.

town or country, engaged at their chosen profession o r prosecuting their studies at p u b l i c schools and colleges, were now — not what t h e y w e r e t o b e g i n with, an unshapen mass of raw material, a nondescript army of undrilled, undisciplined, u n - armed men with nothing but the *will* to do—but an army, equipped

MOTOR SCOUTS OF THE WESTMORLAND AND CUMBERLAND YEOMANRY RIDING AT FULL SPEED.

and ready in every detail to face even the German legions, Infantry of the line, Cavalry, Artillery, Engineers, Royal Army Medical Corps, Army Service Corps, guns, arms, munitions, stores—everything. Nothing overlooked, everything efficient—as efficient as any Regular Army that has ever left the shores of Great Britain. The new Army came into existence with a rush, its training was undertaken and completed with strenuous urgency, everyone knew he was working against time, the essence of the whole endeavour was to be ready by a given date. But efficiency went hand in hand with urgency; everything that was done was done with calculated thoroughness; the soul of the work was Kitchener, and Kitchener stands for thoroughness.

From every walk of life, from the labourers and artisans to the professional men, the public school men, and the nobility, the ranks of the raw new Army were filled. The men who had the training of the recruits worked miracles with this raw material literally thrown at them. But it could not have been done had the goodwill, the good humour, and the abounding enthusiasm of the eager masses been lacking. Full of confidence and vigour, they trained for the joy of training. It was patriotism first that led them to join the colours, then a feverish pride of British determination and tenacity took hold of them—what they had undertaken to do they *would* do. The memory of the things these young men have done will go down to

THE SPORTMAN'S BATTALION MARCHING TO THEIR CAMP AT HORNCHURCH.

generations of Britons yet unborn as a glorious example of British patriotism.

Great Britain has never been a military nation, but when, late in her history, the

SIGNALLING INSTRUCTION IN THE CAP OF THE NEW 1ST LONDON MACHINE GUN BATTERY.

need arose, the eagerness of the youth and the ripe manhood of this country quickly responded, and she became a military nation of the first importance.

Surely the creation of this new Army of millions was an astounding achievement. No less so was the clothing and equipping of them; as with men, so it was with material; we found, after the first few months of recruiting, that the difficulty of obtaining men was as nothing to the difficulty of supplying those men with the necessary equipment. Though arms factories were working day and night, they could not keep up with the demand. But rifles and guns were not the only necessities for the new soldier. His uniform, his boots, his equipment, his underclothes— all these had to be provided, and the factories grappled with the situation resolutely.

The whole country was animated by a desire to help. Whether it was helping Kitchener battalions or whether it was helping our Allies mattered very little so long

as something was being contributed to the common cause. The makers of motor-cars and motor-cycles were so heavily engaged that many of them were obliged to cease supplying civilian customers altogether. Sheffield, instead of manufacturing silver-plate goods, worked seven days a week to provide the Army with its bayonets and its steel-ware; Wol- mingham provided small arms and high explosives; the mills of Huddersfield and Dewsbury worked at full pressure to clothe the Army warmly. Even ladies' dress-makers were hard at work on soldiers' uniforms—you might take the railway guide of England and go through all the great industrial towns, and say of each: "This did something to help forward the great cause."

"We owe," said a member of the Russian commission which visited England in the course of the war, "a very great debt of gratitude to industrial England. It is amazing that, with the Army she is putting in the field, with the great Navy she supports, and with the calls which are made upon her in her oversea wars, that she is able to continue to be as she is—the greatest industrial power in the world."

### The Man who Planned it

The man to whom Great Britain is indebted for the accomplishment of this

A BUGLE COMPANY, 3RD QUEEN VICTORIA'S RIFLES, PRACTISING IN RICHMOND PARK.

verhampton was busy day and night preparing great stocks of leather for harness, saddle, and equipment; the factories of Northampton turned out hundreds of thousands of pairs of boots; Bir- miracle is Lord Kitchener; it was not only to his genius for organisation that the raising of this new Army was possible, but what is even of greater moment, it was Lord Kitchener who at the very outset saw

AT THE DOUBLE – EARLY MORNING PHYSICAL TRAINING.

what the war meant for this country, with only our little Regular Army at her disposal. It was Lord Kitchener who quickly formed what Mr. Bonar Law aptly termed "a gigantic conception" of what military requirements would be necessary to see the thing through, and the *Spectator* very truly observed: "Other men and lesser men,

SOON TO BE MADE SAILORS – 'RAW MATERIAL' ARRIVING AT THE CRYSTAL PALACE.

NAVAL BRIGADE RECRUITS FORMING UP AT THE CRYSTAL PALACE.

even though they might have had enough imagination to see what might and ought to be done, would in the emergency have been daunted by the task before them. They would have argued that it was too late to try any new system, that we were committed to great naval but only to small military action, and that therefore all we could be expected to do, and all we could do, since we were unprepared from the military point of view, was to send abroad a comparatively small but efficient Expeditionary Force, and to keep that force thoroughly equipped and thoroughly well

AS ON BOARD SHIP. – THE HAMMOCKS IN WHICH THE MEN SLEEP.

supplied with men. It is probable that no statesman on either bench would have attempted to do more than keep up the Exeditionary Force and develop the Territorials. Happily, it seemed otherwise to Lord Kitchener. The departure of the first instalments of the Expeditionary Force appeared to leave the military cupboard almost bare. The reserves of equipment and of rifles were, we will not say exhausted, but dangerously reduced by mobilisation. The condition of our arsenals showed that the Government had never contemplated or prepared for a great improvisation of troops, and had been content to shape our military policy wholly on the idea of a moderate-sized Expeditionary Force. Faced with such a situation, Lord Kitchener's was indeed a gigantic, nay, a glorious, conception, and one worthy of the best traditions of the nation.

"To resolve, as Lord Kitchener did, that he would not hear the word 'impossible,' but that at one and the same time he would keep the Expeditionary Force going, double the Territorials, and raise a new Army on a scale to which the history of war affords no parallel, was worthy of Chatham himself. We cannot say more."

It must always be borne in mind that not only had the two millions of men required to be found by voluntary enlistment, but equipment of every conceivable description had to be made. "Men more flighty and with less strength of judgment," continued the *Spectator*, "might have argued : 'It is no good to think of beginning to manufacture machines, to manufacture rifles six months hence. The war may be over by then. What we must do is to concentrate upon the needs of the next six weeks.' Lord Kitchener was fortunately a man capable of taking long views. He was not depressed. He made up his mind that the war would be a long war, and therefore it was worth while to prepare machinery which would only begin to give practical results six months hence. He was not content with wild efforts at jerrybuilding, but determined that his corner-stones should be well and truly laid. Accordingly he began the tremendous task of arraying the manhood of the nation for war, and of developing, organising, and exploiting its great commercial resources for the provision of rifles, machine-guns, great guns, ammunition small and great, clothes and equipment, bayonets and swords, and all the thousand things needed by an army from huts to tents, from waterproofs to field-glasses, from saddles to motor-cars. The Roman Senate thanked their General because he had not despaired of the Republic. Well may we thank ours because last August he not only did not despair of the Republic in the abstract, but also did not despair of the Republic's power to give us men, and also of its power to improvise the equipment for those men. Once more,—'a gigantic conception,' and one which the country is not likely to forget."

I have so far dealt only with the men of Kitchener's Army. While they were being trained, our Territorial Army and our Yeomanry had welcomed the chance of proving their worth. In the next and concluding number I will tell the story of their rally to the flag and how the Empire made use of them at home and abroad.

AT THE CRYSTAL PALACE – DRILLING ON THE FAMOUS FOOTBALL GROUND.

WESTMORLAND AND CUMBERLAND YEOMANRY AT FIELD MANOEUVRES.

## CHAPTER VI

### HOW THE TERRITORIALS ANSWERED THE CALL—SPECIAL REGIMENTS— THE TRAINING OF THE NEW OFFICERS.

FEW people in England, and nobody on the Continent, fully realised that all the time Kitchener's Army was in course of creation yet another force, already in being, was growing by the side of it, employing exactly the same methods of training, and differing so little in appearance as to be mistaken by the uninitiated for the regular soldier. This was the Territorial Army. We may hope that when the war is over some method will be discovered for honouring the men who not only went willingly to the service of the country, but had for many years been devoting their spare time to preparation for the inevitable conflict.

Evolved by Lord Haldane when he was Minister of War from the old Volunteer Army, the Territorials numbered roughly, on the outbreak of war, some 10,000 officers and 250,000 men. They had been attending camp, some of them for many years, were conversant with all the drill, ceremonial and practical, associated with military training; but since they had not been working together continuously, it was inevitable that they lacked something of the *moral* and the tone of the professional soldier. Their mobilisation came at an opportune moment. The order arrived at a time when the annual camps were breaking up, and the Territorials had only sufficient time to go home and arrange their affairs before they were again speeding back to the point of concentration. This time the mobilisation had a new and stern significance.

No longer was it the annual outing, to which city men went with a feeling that, however hard they might work, they were going to get a lot of fun out of their experience; but it was, they knew, to the grim work of real war that they would be asked to direct their attention.

#### The Call to "Imperial Service"

This view of the business at hand was more than confirmed when Lord Kitchener called for volunteers for service abroad. Under the terms of his enlistment the Territorial does not undertake to serve out of the British Isles, but no sooner had the question been put to him than he gave his answer, and it was an answer practically unanimous. The whole of this splendid force — half-trained, it is true, but well equipped and armed and complete in every respect with its artillery, engineers and medical service—offered itself for duty at whatever point Lord Kitchener thought the Territorials might serve their country best.

General Bethune, the commandant of the Territorial force, is one of the strongest men who has occupied that position, and it has been due to his energetic and fearless management of the force that it reached the point of efficiency at which we found it at

THE INNS OF COURT OFFICERS TRAINING CORPS (THE 'DEVIL'S OWN') TRAINING IN TEMPLE GARDENS

the outbreak of war. How would the Territorial force be employed? That was

THE HANTS REGIMENT HALT BY THE ROADSIDE DURING A THIRTY MILE MARCH IN THE MIDLANDS.

line by the side of its comrades in France, but it seemed unlikely that the authorities would send out men who were not completely trained to confront so highly organised a first line Army as that which Germany had put into the field.

The answer came soon enough, but not too soon for these keen young men, who without hesitation had dropped their lucrative employment and were prepared for whatever task the country put before them. Before I go on to tell the question which every man was asking. It was ready to take its place in the firing the story of how their services were utilised, it may be well to go back to those

early days at Mons, when the British Army, confronted by an enemy five times its size, was conducting the most heroic retreat which history records.

We had at that time in the field between 80,000 and 100,000 men, in itself a remarkable achievement. The mobilisation of our available forces had been quite as rapid as that of Germany's. This may seem absurd to any person who does not examine all the circumstances. We had had to call to the colours about 140,000 of the Army Reserve, and these were grouped to some 70 infantry battalions, 14 cavalry regiments, 8 Guards' infantry regiments, 7 brigades of Royal Horse Artillery and 33 brigades of the Royal Field Artillery, with 6 heavy batteries and siege gun companies of the Royal Garrison Artillery. The line regiments as they were could not take the field without their reserves, nor would any prudent War Minister despatch troops until the last man of the very final battalion was ready for the field.

Overseas in India we had 9 cavalry regiments, about 50 infantry battalions, 5 brigades of Royal Horse Artillery, and 15 brigades of Royal Field Artillery, with heavy guns and mounted batteries. In Egypt and the Soudan we had cavalry regiments, a Guards' infantry battalion, 4 line battalions and 1 battery of horse artillery. At Gibraltar, Malta and Hong Kong we had 9 or 10 infantry battalions, to which may be added the 4 cavalry regiments, 11 infantry battalions, a brigade of Royal Horse Artillery and 2 brigades of Royal Field Artillery in North China and the Colonies.

All these were first line troops, vitally necessary, as the events following Mons proved, for the strengthening of the Army which was contributing to the salvation of Europe. Splendid as our Territorials were, they could not compare with these seasoned battalions which were kicking their heels in far-away corners of the globe.

Roughly, there were 76,000 infantrymen alone, all first line troops, who were stationed abroad. And stationed abroad for a considerable period they must have remained had the Territorial force failed to appreciate the seriousness of the situation or slackened in their patriotism. It was to relieve a very large number of these 76,000 that a corresponding or possibly a greater number of Territorials were despatched. Their training, in England at any rate, was brief. So carefully were all the preliminary arrangements made and so well organised was the Army system that

A DETACHMENT RECEIVING INSTRUCTION IN SEMAPHORE SIGNALLING.

THE 3RD BATTALION CITY OF LONDON ROYAL FUSILIERS IN A MIMIC BATTLE.

none saw the going of the Territorial or knew that he was on his way to the strange, sun-washed lands on the other side of the world, to replace his regular comrades at the outposts of Empire.

Without any fuss, without the playing of bands or cheering crowds in the streets, the Territorial force melted away from England. Great white transports took them on board at Southampton and Portsmouth, and they slipped down the Solent, and the people on the shore, who heard the far-away roar of cheers which came from the ship, could only conjecture that these were more men departing for the front. Yet those who had field-glasses could see that this troopship was crowded with men in helmets—great solar topees—and they might suppose that somewhere in the hold of the ship were huge bales of real khaki, thin twill into which the men would change when the troopship had passed through the Red Sea on its way to Bombay. Line after line of transports crossed the Bay of Biscay, some-times escorted by French, sometimes by British, warships, passed through the Straits of Gibraltar—a few remained there to land a new garrison—into the Mediterranean; stop-ping again at Malta, where ship after ship discharged its human cargo; on to Suez, to Aden, to Bombay, to Colombo, to Madras and Calcutta. One ship at least went as far afield as China. Others moved westward to Bermuda and Jamaica, where British forces were garrisoned.

And presently the liners began to return again, laden with brown-faced men, hardened to war—the Tommy Atkins of the Regular Army; relieved from the scene of his inaction, impatient to meet Europe's great enemy. New and strange batteries went trundling through the streets of Indian towns; fresh-faced English boys, sharp-featured Scots—there were many Territorial batteries in Scotland—men from Galway and Clare, Cork and Ulster — especially Ulster — looked curiously at the strange new scenes which were being unfolded before their eyes, and the Indians who squatted at their stalls in the bazaars may well have marvelled at this new evidence of inexhaustible strength which the British Raj was displaying.

"The British Territorials are streaming over the face of India," wrote an Anglo-Indian. "I am meeting the most unlikely people in the most unlikely places."

There was a battery which had its headquarters in Chichester, and probably dreamed of no greater adventure than its annual visit to Okehampton. When last I heard of it, it was sitting tight at Peshawur, that paradise of spring flowers, in the very shadow of the great mountains and on the edge of the land which the Pathan has lorded for hundreds of years.

And now, and not until now, did the Territorial begin his training. Surely no Army unit ever conducted its preparations for war in such picturesque circumstances Though war was re-

TRAINING 'BARRACKS' OF THE 3RD BATTALION H.A.C. – 'MOUNT FELIX,' WALTON-ON-THAMES. THE BANQUETING HALL AS SLEEPING AND GENERAL QUARTERS.

mote enough, though India or Bermuda or China—wherever he found himself—gave him, happily enough, no hope of

THE HONOURABLE ARTILLERY COMPANY ON PARADE AT HEADQUARTERS SHOWING ON RIGHT THE ARMOURY WITH THE REGIMENTAL FLYING FLAG.

no *dolce far niente* for the man of the Territorial Army serving abroad. It was a full and strenuous life which he lived, but he was none the worse for that. The novelty of his surroundings was in itself some reward for his patriotism, and he brought to his new experience the *naïveté* which made for delighted surprise.

"What the natives cannot understand," wrote one Territorial stationed in the heart of India, "is why they brought us out and sent the others home. We interpret this in a complimentary sense, as indicating the very little difference in physique and smartness which can be seen between ourselves and the men of the Regular Army. None of our men, however, has any illusions on the subject; and though we are bitterly disappointed that we cannot go into the field and that we shall probably be rusticating here for twelve months, we are satisfied that the best men have been taken for the job, and we must endeavour as far as possible to fit ourselves, so that we in turn may be numbered with the best."

This was the spirit which animated the splendid force which General Bethune commanded.

Did the Territorials but know, they had not left war behind until they had passed through the Suez Canal. The men of the Territorial forces who were landed at Suez

armed conflict, yet he went into training just as completely as his brethren in England. There was

THE 5TH GLOUCESTERS PRACTISING A CHARGE WITH FIXED BAYONETS NEAR CHELMSFORD.

and at Alexandria, and went into camp under the shadow of the Pyramids, were to see war much sooner than their comrades of Kitchener's Army. Turkey had committed an act of war, and already her columns were mobilising on the Sinai Peninsula for an advance upon Egypt.

To meet this advance and to prepare himself for the inevitable battle, the Territorial joined himself with the newly arrived Australians who had come to the aid of the Motherland, and had been disembarked at Suez, in fitting himself physically and "regimentally" on the spot.

A BATTERY OF THE HONOURABLE ARTILLERY IN CAMP.

A FIELD TELEPHONE OPERATOR OF THE GLOUCESTER TERRITORIALS COMMUNICATING INFORMATION TO HEADQUARTERS.

the French Fleet had been invited to use Malta as their base. There was a coming and going of warships, transports, great liners, destroyers and submarines, and, we may be sure, a storing on a large scale of ammunition for the Navy, which it was the duty of the Territorial to guard. Here he must use his wits and must exercise unceasing vigilance, for Malta is cosmopolitan in character, and certain neutrals are to be found here in great strength. He had to learn the value of taciturnity and become in a way a miniature diplomatist. For the secrets which a private of the Territorials may reveal a great German General may use to his own advantage.

In Egypt the Empires met. Lithe and active Indian troops, sinewy Australians, those pink and white Territorial boys—now growing hard of thew and mahogany of face under cloudless skies—these, with a sprinkling of regular troops which had been left for the purpose, began to make hard the way of the invader. It is not my purpose in this publication to describe the first great Turkish attack and the disastrous consequences which attended our enemy on that occasion. It is sufficient to say that the Territorial proved himself upon that field to be a first-class fighting man, worthy of his high calling.

In Malta great events were going forward, in which the Territorial took his part. Malta is on the high road to the East, one of the busiest "roadways" of the world, and it gained in liveliness from the fact that

Doubtless from Malta he saw all the preparations which were being made for the bombardment of the Dardanelles; since the preparations for this, one of the decisive and certainly one of the most brilliant achievements of the war, must have been made at this great naval base.

The Territorial who found himself at Gibraltar had less excitement, and was even denied the fun which in normal times of peace could be found in an occasional visit to the Spanish territory across the neutral ground.

### Special Regiments

Associated with the Territorial movement is a large number of Yeomanry regiments, all of which volunteered for service in other lands. It is not too much to say that the Yeomanry of England were amongst the best trained of the purely volunteer troops. In the main these forces are made up of countrymen, healthy, vigorous disciples of outdoor life and field sports, and having a lifelong acquaintance with that "friend of man" who is the terror of the cavalry recruit. It is a notable fact that a

OFFICERS OF THE BEDFORDSHIRE REGIMENT SNATCHING A HASTY LUNCH DURING AN INTERVAL ON A FIELD-DAY.

Yeomanry regiment was the first of the Territorials engaged in the great war, its services having been specially referred to by Field-Marshal Sir John French. If it was the first, others soon followed. Not all the Territorials were taken for service in India

THE CIVIL SERVICE RIFLES, 15TH COUNTY OF LONDON, ON A ROUTE MARCH.

being fit to take their place in the fighting line, the names of the London Scottish, the Artists' Rifles, the Honourable Artillery Company, and the Suffolk Regiment occur to me.

Of the Honourable Artillery Company, which stands first among Territorial corps by reason of its ancient beginnings, much has been written. It is the pride of the Company, which includes infantry units bearing the same relation to the Territorial battalions as the Brigade of Guards does to the infantry of the line, that it is ready at all times for war. This is probably not quite accurate in fact,

and the Colonies. Of the Territorial corps which rendered good service in France, and were regarded by the military authorities as though it is certain that the discipline and the efficiency of the Corps are of a very high order.

THE SECOND BATTALION OF THE LONDON SCOTTISH IN TRAINING.

The units I have mentioned rendered an excellent account of themselves, and the following were also spoken of in General French's third despatch :—The Northumberland, Northamptonshire, North Somerset, Leicester, and Oxfordshire Regiments of Yeomanry, and the Hertfordshire and Queen's Westminster Battalions of Territorial Infantry.

"The conduct and bearing of these units under fire," said Sir John French, "and the efficient manner in which they have carried out the various duties assigned to them, have imbued me with the highest hope as to the value and help of the Territorial troops generally."

Everybody has heard of the exploits of the London Scottish, whilst a company of the 4th Suffolk Regiment, a Territorial corps recruited entirely in Ipswich and the neighbourhood about, did splendid work at the taking of Givenchy. Indeed, this exploit may be described as one of the most brilliant feats of the war. The enemy had come down, driven out the troops who held the trenches to the east of the village, and had seized upon the village itself, organising it for defence. The German advance had been so unexpected and his success so

unforeseen, that for the moment it seemed that he would jeopardise the whole of the British line. An army corps which had been in reserve was hurried forward to grapple with the situation, and in the meantime the Manchester Regiment and a company of the 4th Suffolks delivered a furious counter-attack in face of outnumbering odds, and, in spite of the fact that they were met by a most terrible concentration of rifle and machine-gun fire, they seized one end of the village and held their position until the relieving corps came up to complete the German discomfiture.

It is in reason that there should be an inequality of efficiency in regiments which have only one opportunity in the course of a year to exercise together. Much depends upon opportunities for meeting, upon whether the corps has already acquired some traditions, and generally upon its composition. Some regiments are especially favoured in that all the companies are drawn from a restricted area. In other cases there are company headquarters at towns wide apart, and, save at the annual training, men have no opportunity of meeting and harmonising one with the other.

It is because such regiments as the

London Scottish are recruited in one city, and the members of the corps meet generally once a week, that the regiment has always been a coherent force. Corps which consisted of scattered units suffered in consequence; but the war brought them all together, and such of those as were regarded by the War Office as likely and suitable men for active service were put to the real hard work of training which distinguished Kitchener's Army in its preliminary stages.

The active service Territorials—that is to say, the men who were ear-marked for work in France—had the advantage of the

THE LONDON SCOTTISH LINING UP FOR ROLL-CALL AFTER THEIR MEMORABLE CHARGE AT MESSINES.

2ND BATTALION LONDON SCOTTISH MARCHING DOWN LUDGATE HILL IN THE LORD MAYOR'S PROCESSION.

Kitchener troops in that they had a thorough grounding in one side of soldiering. They knew their weapons, they knew how to march; the elements of drill had already been instilled into them; and they started their work a month ahead of their great rivals. For this reason they were employed earlier, and, long before Kitchener's Army had sailed for France, half-a-dozen Territorial units had made their mark in the field.

The criticism has been passed that the Territorial did not mix readily either with the Kitchener soldier or with the Regular. But this is a view which was rather based upon the attitude of the two arms in pre-war days than on the situation which the war revealed.

It was an unfortunate fact that, by the system in vogue before the war, the Territorials were only identified with the regiment whose name they bore by the fact that they wore the same badge and that they were called fifth or sixth battalions of that regiment. Communion between the Regular and the Territorial there was not. It was not due on the one side to apathy, or on the other to lack of interest.

It merely was that there existed no channel of communication between the regular battalions and their amateur friends. This is a condition of affairs which, one can confidently hope, will be remedied at the conclusion of the war.

Another Territorial battalion to which reference should be made is the Artists' Rifles. The Artists' Rifles enjoyed the unique distinction of being converted on the field of battle into an officers training corps. Classes were formed from chosen men of the regiments, and these, under able instructors, were detailed for actual work in the trenches, examined upon their observations and upon the knowledge they had acquired at first hand, and were drafted with commissions to various regular regiments serving at the front. It says much for the high standard which the Artists' Rifles have been able to maintain for many years that a Territorial regiment should enjoy the honour of supplying from its private members commissioned officers for the Regular Army.

To sum up the achievements of the Territorial Force, it can be said that they showed a remarkable efficiency and a zeal and patriotism beyond all praise. Territorial units were scattered all over the world; they were brought to face the Turks in Egypt, to hold the marches of the wild Indian border; they were thrown into the sodden trenches of Flanders; they guarded the railways of England, and were amongst the watchers of the coast who kept our shores against surprise raids. At home and abroad, unostentatiously and thoroughly, they worked with a will at whatever task was assigned them, and they earned for themselves, their regiments, and the Territorial movement a fame which will not die so long as the memory of the war lasts.

SCOUTS OF THE HERTS YEOMANRY LOCATING THE ENEMY.

It should be recorded that, just as in the case of Kitchener's Army, the Territorial Force received admirable help from employers. Every man of the Territorial Army was, one is safe in saying, in regular and fairly well paid employment. The majority were men with wives and families, upon whom would devolve a great deal of hardship by the withdrawal of their breadwinner. It was the employer of labour, with his system of half salary or even better, who saw that the men of the Territorial Army went to their far-off duties with the happy feeling that their wives and families were well provided for.

Here, too, a tribute should be paid to the

QUEEN'S WESTMINSTERS MARCH FROM LONDON TO WATFORD – THE PHOTOGRAPH SHOWS THEM FALLING IN AFTER A SHORT HALT.

ARMY SERVICES CORPS SECTION OF LONDON TERRITORIALS RETURNING TO CAMP AT SALISBURY PLAIN AFTER BIVOUACKING ALL NIGHT.

work of the Territorial Committees, who, acting under the Lord Lieutenant of the county from which the battalion was drawn, did so much, not only in assisting the battalion to fit itself for service, but in guarding the interests of the men while they were at the Front. In some cases—indeed, in many cases—these Territorial Associations spent large sums of money upon the battalions. Not only are we indebted to the Territorial Committees for the efficiency, but for the very recruitment of the men.

At the outbreak of war recruiting for Territorial battalions was one of the features of an electric month. That recruitment, however, was more or less

THE ARTISTS' RIFLES MARCHING PAST THE SALUTING POINT AT A REVIEW BY H.M. THE KING. MANY OF THE MEMBERS OF THE REGIMENT HAVE BEEN GIVEN COMMISSION IN THE REGULAR FORCES.

stopped when the urgent need became apparent for bringing the Kitchener masses into line. There could be no longer any diffusion of effort, and the attention of recruiters was concentrated upon bringing service battalions into existence.

After the Regular battalions on foreign service had been relieved, and after the defences of Egypt had been strengthened and the fitter Territorial battalions placed in the field, General Bethune might with justice have said: "The Territorial Force has done its share; it is now the turn of Kitchener's Army."

### The Training of the Officers

I have reserved to the last this very important chapter on the training of the officer. That it could be left to the end of this publication is due to the fact that the training was identical both in Kitchener's Army and in the Territorial regiments. I do not purpose following the young officer who was joining such technical corps as the Royal Engineers or the Royal Field Artillery, or any of the associate Territorial batteries. These corps call for special qualities and special knowledge. The young officer who was gazetted to the artillery branches must be well up in mathematics, and must, did he wish to be of any value to his new service, possess an aptitude for the work which he was undertaking.

For him, too, it was necessary that he should be trained very much the same as a cavalry recruit is trained in

THE ARTISTS' RIFLES PARADING PREPARATORY TO THEIR THREE DAYS MARCH TO ALDERSHOT, WHERE THEY WENT FOR TRAINING AT EASTER.

the riding school; for, even if he were an accomplished rider, he was to learn that the Army way differed in a very considerable degree from that happy-go-lucky method of riding with which he was familiar. We will leave the artillery officer to his gun drill, to his trigonometry and his wonderful calculations, and we will deal with the Kitchener officer proper—that is to say, the young man who applied for a commission and was drafted to one of the infantry battalions.

We may also dismiss the old infantry officer who had left the Army and in some cases had gone abroad, who returned at the first hint of war to offer his sword to the War Office. He found himself, even though he were a subaltern when he left the Army, promoted to a rank above his wildest dreams in times of peace; and upon him lay the authority of establishing the "spirit" of a regiment. In the Continental armies there are *cadres*—skeleton forces of non-commissioned officers and officers —around which new formations may be grouped. These form a nucleus or a skeleton for new troops. In the British Army no *cadres* existed. Yet such was the spirit in which we met this war that, hardly had the new recruits begun to form, than *cadres* appeared as if by magic, and the new-born regiment discovered its routine.

Two thousand officers were called for at the beginning of the war, and 20,000 men applied for commissions. Since then more than 50,000, and probably

THE LONDON RIFLES BRIGADE IN CAMP.

nearer 100,000, new officers were absorbed into the Army. The qualifications necessary and the tests, both social and educational, which were applied in time of peace were heavy and searching, and, although one may imagine many officers secured commissions after the outbreak of war, and secured them without any preliminary examination or without any other credentials than the recommendation

THE BISHOP OF LONDON HOLDING A SERVICE IN THE CAMP OF THE LONDON RIFLE BRIGADE.

of the head of a public school, supported or endorsed by an officer of the Army (generally one commanding a regiment or depôt), there were surprisingly few misfits admitted to the regimental messrooms.

When the young officer received an intimation that he had been gazetted to a regiment, he was instructed to report himself on a certain day to the officer commanding, and he was given a warrant, which is equivalent to a railway ticket, to proceed to his destination. His introduction to his new colonel was often, for the officer recruit,

hurst and at Woolwich the courses which are set for applicants for commissions were continued as though nothing was happening. The leisurely preparation of the young Sandhurst boy, not for the war but for the conditions which would follow the war, illustrated the calm confidence of the British people, and was, in fact, the evidence of "Business as Usual" in the Army.

A second system was found at the great universities and public schools which had officers training corps attached. Here young men paid fairly large fees and

SURREY YEOMANRY WATERING THEIR HORSES.

a very trying and embarrassing experience, for he was conscious in many cases that he was wholly unacquainted with the customs of Army life. He was a fortunate man if he came straight from an officers training corps, for then at least he would have had a grounding in the rudiments of his craft.

Whilst war was in progress several systems of officers training were going on. First, and most important, was the training of the officer who was intended for continuous service with the Army—that is to say, after the war was concluded. At Sand-

supported themselves during the process of their training, until they reached the point of proficiency at which they might be recommended for admission to some of the crack corps of the Army for the duration of the war. Their instruction included all that the recruit private learned, including a very complete training in the use of arms. In addition, there were long lectures on tactical and strategical subjects, field operations and tactical schemes. In other words, the would-be officer was taught methods for attacking or defending certain positions and was given command of wholly mythical troops, and was expected to manœuvre those troops on a sham battlefield to the satisfaction of his mentor. Field sketching and reconnaissance work were part of the curriculum.

The would-be officer who, if he were a University man, would have at least some knowledge of drawing, was sent to reduce the topography of a strange country to paper. He must be a perfect judge of distances, must, with the aid of his compass, be able to trace the direction of roads and the character of railways, must set

down, so that his chief to whom he communicated his report would be able to read without any risk of mistake, the presence of swamps, woods and defensive positions scribbled on the roughly made map. The instructor did not spare him, and he must make long marches and endure the discomforts which he would be asked to endure when he was attached to a regiment and had to handle men.

Moreover, the coming officer was required to gain a working knowledge of military law. Military law differs very little from civil law, save that it imposes punishments for offences which are unknown in the civil code. That a man who shamefully casts away his arms or abandons his position in the face of the enemy, or commits acts of treachery towards his comrades, is liable to the penalty of death, he knew. But it was the minor crime and its exact importance, together with the punishment which should be awarded, which puzzled him a little.

"Crime" in the Army is a term applied to any lapse or failing on the part of a private soldier. It is a crime not to shave; it is a crime to be absent-minded and fail to carry out an order. Slackness and slovenliness; absence beyond the allowed hours of leave; impertinence to a superior officer, by

AN OXFORD LIGHT INFANTRYMAN SOUNDING A BUGLE CALL.

which is meant a non-commissioned officer; talking in the ranks; wearing long hair after being warned to have it cut: all these things are in military jargon "crimes," each calling for a different form of punishment.

The young officer was merely learning the theory of it all. He would not be called upon to award punishment until he had had a very considerable experience in regi-

HANTS CYCLISTS, LED BY CAPTAIN LOW.

mental work. It was the company officer who marked the man's defaulter's sheet. Nor would he be asked to grapple with the involved question of the soldiers' pay. Yet for a would-be officer, the preparation of military accounts was not the least important of his duties.

He must make himself completely acquainted with the soldier's kit and his method of carrying it. He must learn from wise instructors something of the complexities of a soldier's mind. Mostly was he taught that there was a time for everything, and that he would best gain the confidence of his men and inspire their respect by a certain aloofness, a certain remoteness, save in extraordinary circumstances.

"I want you to understand," said the speaker at one of the lectures I attended, "that if you go into the Army with the idea of introducing some new method or some new system for improving its character, you are going to have a very unpleasant time. If you go to work ostentatiously to gain the confidence of your men, you will merely arouse their suspicion or their contempt. British soldiers do not want mothering, they want leading; and to be led properly they must have complete confidence in their leader. All soldiers have grievances: it is their legitimate possession. And if you wander round looking for grievances you will find six in every tent, providing there are six people sleeping there. The more people who live in the tent, the more grievances you will find. It is an Army saying that to 'grouse' is the soldier's privilege.

"You must, too, be careful in dealing with

THE ROYAL SCOTS FUSILIERS IN TRAINING NEAR BASINGSTOKE.

MEMBERS OF THE INNS OF COURT OFFICERS' TRAINING CORPS (THE 'DEVILS OWN') PRACTISE SIGNALLING IN LINCOLN'S INN FIELDS.

a non-commissioned officer. Remember that he knows a great deal more about the business of soldiering than you do or than you will for a very long time. He will salute you and pay you every mark of respect, but for quite a while his mental attitude towards you will be one of derision and pity. Remember that if you catch a non-commissioned officer napping once, you must keep the fact to yourself. The joyous impulse to correct the N.C.O. before his men, if given way to, will induce him on some future occasion to correct you by inference, because you may be sure that for every mistake he makes you will make twenty. Do not be familiar with the non-commissioned officer in order to gain his approval, because the result will be the reverse to what you desire. Remember that it is your business to maintain the discipline of the regiment, and the best disciplined regiments are invariably the best fighting regiments.

"You have to set your mind on arriving in the trenches, where you will be all men together, so firmly established in their esteem and regard, that if you were suddenly reduced to

the rank of a private and the men were called upon to elect their officers, they would elect you among them. Soldiers do not want you for your geniality, and they will not prize you for your graciousness. They recognise that it is your business to lead, and to show them the way in or the way out whenever circumstances call upon you for the exercise of your judgment. If you fail them in their hour of need, or show weakness at a moment when strength is required of you, you are finished and done with.

"Remember also that the soldier's highest term of praise is: 'Mr. So-and-so is a gentleman'; and let that always be in your mind when you are on leave and you are meeting soldiers of every kind at the corner of every street. When the soldier salutes you, will you please remember that he is not saluting Mr. Johnson or Mr. Brown, nor is he saluting the well-cut uniform you wear, but he is saluting the King's commission which, in theory, is neatly folded up in your breast-pocket? The salute to the officer is a

SCOUTS OF THE HERTS YEOMANRY AT WORK.

salute to the King, and if you fail to acknowledge that salute, or take it as for yourself, you are acting carelessly, not alone to the soldier whose salute you have ignored or only carelessly acknowledged, but to the King whose commission you carry.

"One other point I would make, and that has reference to your behaviour in the field. It is expected of you that you will be brave under all circumstances; but you have also to remember that the Government has taken a lot of trouble with you, and will be paying you a much larger salary than it pays to

he was gazetted in the glory of print, he at least went to his new comrades well founded in wisdom. Between theory and practice there is a very wide gulf, and the young officer might find some difficulty in applying all the wise sayings which had been instilled into his mind to the actualities which he found around him.

The consensus of opinion, both in Kitchener's Army and in the Territorial Army, was that the new officer who had come forward was of first-class quality. And here it may be said that the Army chiefs had to exercise the very wisest dis-

MAXIM GUN SECTION OF THE NORTHUMBERLAND HUSSARS.

the private soldier in order that you should carry out certain duties. Unnecessary exposure is not heroic but foolish. Always remember that once you are dead you are no use in the Army. A famous French General of the Napoleonic war spoke of an officer who had lost his life in a particularly foolhardy expedition that he had 'deserted to heaven.' I would like you to keep that in your minds."

I have given this little condensation of a lecture to illustrate the moral training of the young aspirant of the officers training corps. When his commission arrived and

cretion in granting commissions to men. The tradition of the British Army is that the ranker does not inspire confidence. It is equally true that the British soldier is more exigent even than his Prussian foeman in his demand for the "well born." The great public schools of England contributed almost to their last man to the call for officers. The Universities were denuded of students to provide additional men for that corps. Over 7,000 Cambridge men, new and old, were serving with the colours in February, 1915, and Oxford had sent as many. The technical and science colleges,

AUSTRALIAN CAVALRY AT THE SPHINX – BRITISH TERRITORIALS HAVE ALSO BEEN SENT TO EGYPT.

like those at Birmingham and at Durham, have been responsible for large drafts to the Royal Engineers, as well as to the line battalions.

When the new officer came from officers training corps, or when he was graduated from such units as the Artists' Rifles in the manner I have described in a previous chapter, it was all smooth sailing for the Board of Selection. The difficulty came when papers of recommendation arrived, endorsed by the head of a school, and recommended other than by officers commanding training corps. The commission was often granted, and the young man, who was an absolute tyro to the Army, was sent to a battalion to drill in the recruits' squad and gradually to reach the same stage of efficiency at which his men were aiming. It is a matter for national pride that we made

THE CAMP OF THE BRITISH TROOPS, INCLUDING TERRITORIALS, ON THE TURKISH SIDE OF THE SUEZ CANAL.

TERRITORIALS HAVE BEEN SENT TO REPLACE REGULAR TROOPS IN EGYPT, MALTA, GIBRALTAR, AND INDIA. THE ABOVE PHOTOGRAPH SHOWS SOME OF THE MEN ON ACTIVE SERVICE OVERSEAS.

very few mistakes, and that of the enormous numbers of officers who joined, a remarkably small number proved to be useless for the purpose.

The Government was most generous in its treatment of new officers, granting them a liberal allowance for their kit and giving them pay on a scale which enabled them to live fairly comfortably without drawing upon their private incomes or upon the incomes of their relatives.

It helped considerably to maintain the proper spirit in the Army that the war had been a subalterns' war, and that the junior officers had distinguished themselves and gained honour in the performance of their duties. The splendid young men whose names were constantly occurring in the lists

of decorations awarded by the King urged the new officers forward in a spirit of emulation.

The new officers took themselves and their work very seriously indeed, and their task was made the smoother by the knowledge that, if they were new to the game, so also were the soldiers they were called upon to command. They grew up side by side, officer and man, tackling their difficult and dangerous jobs with an admirable regard for all that depended upon them.

They imbibed the traditions of the regiment to which they were attached, and grew immensely jealous of those traditions. The Kitchener officer and the Territorial officer were worthy of their men. No higher praise than this could be bestowed.

THE END

# Epilogue

A British attack on the Somme through a cloud of poisonous gas. Note the different styles of gas mask, with the British soldiers wearing a hood type.

British troops advance under the cover of a screen of smoke bombs.

A soldier uses a periscope to look out of the British trenches on the Somme. These simple devices avoided the risk of attracting the attention of the enemy snipers.

On the Somme the constant artillery bombardment had stripped the trees to bare stumps. The remains of 'Des Fermes' woods are shown in this photograph.

In the British trenches on the front line, these soldiers keep watch amid a scene of utter devastation within 100 yards of Thiepval.

Behind the lines, sorting the huge quantities of mail from home.

The cavalry lines on the Somme in September 1916.

Outside Taunton railway station, a gun tractor and heavy gun have likely just arrived to be transported by rail after exercises.

THE FIRST WORLD WAR IN PHOTOGRAPHS

# 1914

## OVER BY CHRISTMAS

JOHN CHRISTOPHER & CAMPBELL McCUTCHEON

1914: The First World War in Photographs

John Christopher & Campbell McCutcheon

1914: the first year of the 'war to end all wars'. The First World
War changed the art of war forever; here the authors document the
horrors of war in the photographs of those times.

978 1 4456 2181 4
176 pages, illustrated throughout

Available from all good bookshops or order direct
from our website www.amberley-books.com

THE FIRST WORLD WAR IN PHOTOGRAPHS

# 1915

## SETBACKS & FAILURES

JOHN CHRISTOPHER & CAMPBELL McCUTCHEON

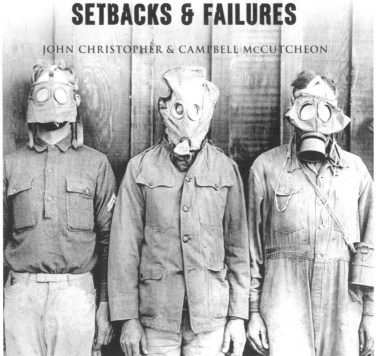

1915: The First World War in Photographs

John Christopher & Campbell McCutcheon

1915, the second year of the Great War, was to see the failure of
the Dardanelles landings and the sinking of the Lusitania. Here,
the authors tell the story of 1915 at war using many rare and often
unpublished images.

978 1 4456 2205 7
176 pages, illustrated throughout

Available from all good bookshops or order direct
from our website www.amberley-books.com

THE FIRST WORLD WAR IN PHOTOGRAPHS

# 1916

## A WAR OF ATTRITION

JOHN CHRISTOPHER & CAMPBELL McCUTCHEON

1916: The First World War in Photographs

John Christopher & Campbell McCutcheon

1916, the third year of the Great War, was to see the introduction of conscription for the first time in Britain. Here, the authors tell the story of 1916 at war using many rare and often unpublished images.

978 1 4456 2208 8
176 pages, illustrated throughout

Available from all good bookshops or order direct
from our website www.amberley-books.com

THE FIRST WORLD WAR IN PHOTOGRAPHS

# 1917

## MUD AND TANKS

JOHN CHRISTOPHER & CAMPBELL McCUTCHEON

1917: The First World War in Photographs

John Christopher & Campbell McCutcheon

1917, the fourth year of the Great War, saw another year in the trenches for millions of troops mobilised in Europe. Here, the authors tell the story of 1917 at war using many rare and often unpublished images.

978 1 4456 2210 1
176 pages, illustrated throughout

Available from all good bookshops or order direct from our website www.amberley-books.com